THIRSK AT WAR

1939 - 1945

To Kevin, with good wishes
Geoff Moore.

GEOFF MOORE

Published in 2004
by Mole End Publishers
Thirsk

ISBN No. 0-9549038-0-3

Printed and bound by in Great Britain by:
The Max Design & Print Co
Kettlestring Lane, Clifton Moor,
York YO30 4XF

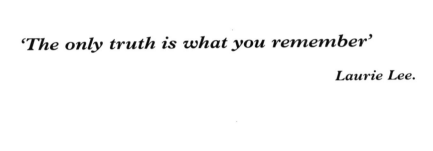

'The only truth is what you remember'

Laurie Lee.

Preface

As in any book of this type a number of sources have been used. The Minutes of Thirsk Rural District Council (T.R.D.C) have been widely quoted, as have extracts from the Darlington and Stockton Times (D/S). A young Neil Graham kept a wartime diary for three years and when used it is referred to as 'diary.' while Elvington Air Museum is noted as (E.A.M.)

Thirsk and its rural area was to witness the building of three additional aerodromes: Topcliffe, Dalton and Skipton-on-Swale. These three, plus Dishforth aerodrome, resulted in a vast increase in traffic and personnel, as well as changes in what was once a familiar landscape. Not only were there real aerodromes with real aeroplanes, but there were also a number of decoy sites at Boltby, Cold Kirby, and Raskelf. The military and those who were conscripted into the Land Army also made an impact, as did the evacuees and prisoners of war.

Many people have shared their time and memories with me and to them I owe a debt of gratitude.

Geoff Moore

Introduction

Europe was not at peace with itself during 1938. The memories of 'the war to end all wars' still lingered. Vivid reminders of the sacrifices made during the 1914 - 1918 conflict could be seen on the war memorials in towns and villages throughout the North Riding of Yorkshire, as in the rest of the country.

Thirsk, and its surrounding parishes, was, just prior to the outbreak of the Second World War, making a slow but determined effort to recover from a slump in agriculture. The town with its markets on Mondays and Saturdays, became a barometer for its prosperity. Here the people from the villages would bring their wares to sell - butter, eggs, rhubarb, beetroot, cheese, onions, peas, cabbages, rabbits, pigeons. They would come by horse and cart, by bus, by motorcar and on foot. Wares would be displayed for the buyers from Leeds, many of them Jews, to handle and to offer such money as they sought fit. It was never enough, but it had to do.

The bustle of the market could not blot out the smoke from the hundreds of chimneys or the noise of the trains as the London and North Eastern Railway plied its trade some one mile to the west of the town. Neither would the smoke blot out the smell from the horse dung and the privies of the dwellings as the people went about their daily lives.

Housing was poor, especially for those who earned little. Yet even the very poor tried to keep clean and respectable, often against impossible odds. The health of the local population was not supported by a supply of good clean water. Wells and pumps were frequently condemned, especially when outbreaks of the dreaded diphtheria and scarlet fever made inroads into family life.

The people of the district were resilient and made their own entertainment. The Ritz and the Regent Cinemas provided a 'Hollywood escape' from the realities of a long working week. Dances, whist drives, socials, an occasional visiting circus added to the leisure pursuits available. Cycles were in demand and those in need of excitement and adventure could watch the motor-cycle climb at Sutton Bank. Gliding, for those who could afford it, was available, as were excursions to Scarborough from Thirsk by train.

Fine weather favoured Thirsk Show which demonstrated a faith in tradition and in the future of agriculture. A rare faith at this particular time, but one that was to be justified by the future.

I.T.M.A. (It's That Man Again.) was first broadcast on the wireless on the 19th September, 1939 with Tommy Handley as the Minister of Aggravation. The years from the outbreak of war until 1945 were indeed to be 'Years of Aggravation'. This account gives a little insight into those years.

Contents

Photographs

CHAPTER ONE
March 1938 to 1939

In spite of assurances from almost every quarter preparations for war went ahead. The Government, following advice, began to prepare the population for a new type of warfare - aerial bombardment. As a result elected Councils throughout the country began to receive directives from Central Government. Thirsk Rural District Council was one of these

28th MARCH 1938 (T.R.D.C.)
Air Raid Precautions.

The Chairman (G.A.Lomas Esq. J.P.) reported that he had received a telegram from the Home Office asking all Local Authorities to proceed with propaganda for the obtaining of volunteers and personnel in regard to Air Raid Precautions Schemes. He also gave a resumé of the proceedings of various meetings and the progress of Schemes in Area No. 5 of the North Riding County Council.

A general discussion took place and the members all agreed to help in the scheme as far as possible.

4th JULY 1938 (T.R.D.C.)
Medical Officer of Health's Report.

The Medical Officer of Health attended and reported on a meeting which had been held by the Medical Officers of Health in regard to Air Raid Precautions and stated that the only suitable building he knew of in this area for casualties was the Isolation Hospital, and asked that consideration be given to this matter when dealing with the hospital.

Isolation Hospital.

The chairman (A.S.C. Broadway Esq.) reported that most of the bedding, etc. had been removed from the Isolation Hospital at Sutton Road, Thirsk, to the Isolation Hospital at Northallerton.

28th SEPTEMBER 1938 (D/S).

Parliament assembled to hear the Prime Minister speak, 'How horrible, fantastic, incredible it is that we should be digging trenches and trying on gas masks here because of a quarrel in a far away country between people of whom we know nothing.'

29th SEPTEMBER 1938

Chamberlain flew to a meeting with Hitler at Munich and terms agreed.

30th SEPTEMBER 1938

Chamberlain, holding up a piece of paper for the cameras announced that Hitler had renounced all war-like intentions against Great Britain. 'I believe it is peace for our time,' the Prime Minister told a cheering crowd in Downing Street later that day.

1st OCTOBER 1938 (D/S)

Take Care of Your Gas Mask if you want it to take care of you.

You may one day owe your life to your gas mask, so treat it with respect The Government are having manufactured special cardboard boxes in which gas masks should be kept and carried about. Until you get yours the chief thing to remember is to avoid bending, creasing or folding the piece of transparent material at the front of the mask. If this should crack or tear it will admit gas.

Your respirator is designed to withstand ordinary use for a long time. Reasonable care must be taken to preserve it in good condition.

You should learn how to put on and take off your respirator. If the proper method is used no damage is likely to be caused when haste is necessary. The respirator should be kept in a cool place away from strong light as exposure to heat and strong light causes deterioration of materials. Your respirator must be dried after use as the inside will be wet from your breath, and it must be dried if exposed to rain. Never carry or hang your respirator by the head straps.

Carry your respirator with you wherever you may be, both night and day, and pay constant attention to keeping it and carrying it so as to avoid damage.

1st OCTOBER 1938

Germans march unopposed into Czechoslovakia.

10th OCTOBER 1938 (T.R.D.C.)

Air Raid Precautions.

A general discussion took place in regard to the above and with a view to expediting the carrying out of a scheme in the area. The following members were appointed to act as Air Raid Precautions Committee with executive powers.

Chairman - G.A.Lomas Esq. J.P.

Rev. A.D. Kevan, Messrs. A.S.C. Broadway, C.C. Forster, E.Reed, L.Ryder.

14th OCTOBER 1938 (T.R.D.C.)

Air Raid Precautions Committee.

Present:-G.A. Lomas Esq. J.P. *(Chairman)*, Messrs. A.S.C. Broadway; J.A. Gott; L. Ryder; Col. C.N. Littleboy, Mr N. Davies; Mr. F. Stockton-Gowland, *(Clerk)*; Dr. W.G. MacArthur, (Medical Officer of Health), Mr. W.A. Wilkinson *(Financial Officer)*, Mr.F.Metcalfe, *(Sanitary Inspector)*.

Apologies for non-attendance were received from Rev. A.D. Kevan and Mr. E. Reed.

A letter was read from Mr. C.C. Forster giving his views on Air Raid Precautions Scheme.

Mr. Davies, (County Air Raid Precautions Officer for the District) gave a resumé of what was required in the area as a guide to the preparation of the Scheme.

The Medical Officer of Health reported that he had received instructions from the County Medical Officer of Health as to the preparations he had to make in regard to First Aid in the area.

He had accordingly arranged for First Aid Posts and Points, together with Depots where First Aid Haversacks would be available. His scheme slightly exceeded that allowed by the County, but the Committee were of the opinion that it was necessary and approved the Medical Officer's action and, at the same time, thanked him for the excellent progress he had made.

After general discussion of the Scheme it was recommended that:-

a) Col. C. N. Littleboy be appointed as Honorary Air Raid Precautions Officer.

b) this Council work in close touch with Wath Rural District Council,

c) the requisite maps be purchased,

d) the Clerk make enquiries as to the appointment of a Clerk for the Honorary Air Raid Precautions Officer and also the provision of the necessary accommodation.

7th NOVEMBER 1938 (T.R.D.C.)

Letter from Stokesley Rural District Council in regard to Evacuation - that in the event of evacuation being necessary, this Council would support them in demanding the setting apart of our districts for the reception of evacuees from the North Riding.

Resolved that this Council support Stokesley Rural District Council.

2nd DECEMBER 1938 (T.R.D.C.)
Dalton and Topcliffe Water Supply.

The Clerk reported that the contractor who was to carry out works on the new aerodrome at Carlton Miniott had approached him with a view to the Council supplying them with water for construction purposes, until such time as the Thirsk and District Water Company could supply them. It was understood that the contractors would do the necessary piping from the Council's main on Topcliffe Station Road. The Clerk had agreed that they be allowed to use not more than 3,000 gallons per day on these terms.

Recommended that the Clerk's decision be approved.

4ᵗʰ December 1938 (T.R.D.C.)

The Medical Officer of Health reported that there was an epidemic of diphtheria in the Parishes of Thirsk and Sowerby. He strongly recommended immunisation of children against diphtheria.

11ᵗʰ December 1938 (T.R.D.C.)

Government Evacuation Scheme.

The Clerk submitted an account amounting to £57-8 2d for surplus emergency rations which had been sold.

Recommended that this account be paid.

Fire Brigade.

The Clerk reported that the extension from Messrs. F. W. Todd and Sons telephone to Mr. J. Todd's house had been completed and the new system of calling the Fire Brigade at nights would be in operation as from Wednesday next.

Salvaging.

The Sanitary Inspector reported that it would be necessary for a shed to be erected for the storing of salvaged scrap metal, paper, etc. at the Destructor.

18ᵗʰ December 1938 (T.R.D.C.)

Letter from the Director of Education and Evacuation Officer of the County Borough of Sunderland, expressing sincere appreciation and thanks to all concerned who welcomed the townsfolk of Sunderland into their homes, and most particularly to those who are devoting themselves to the care of the children.

It was reported that Miss Atkinson, who had voluntarily given a considerable amount of her time to work in connection with the above, had found it necessary to relinquish her duties.

Recommended that a letter of thanks be sent to her in appreciation of the valuable services rendered by her, and that she be paid an honorarium of £5 for this work.

13ᵗʰ January 1939 (T.R.D.C.)

Government Evacuation Scheme

The Clerk submitted circular 1759 of the Ministry of Health to all Local Authorities, stating that arrangements must be planned for such measures of orderly evacuation from the crowded areas of large towns as circumstances may require. The objective must be to secure, by a policy of evacuation carefully planned in advance, the removal from the more dangerous to the less dangerous areas of those whose transfer is most desirable. The survey of accommodation, which is a necessary preliminary step, must of course cover all accommodation which can be used for this purpose.

The first essential measure is to compile an accurate record of all available housing accommodation. It is proposed therefore, to undertake a survey of such accommodation with a view to ascertaining:-

a) the amount of surplus accommodation on the standard of one person per habitable room.
b) the amount of this surplus to be found in houses which are suitable for reception.
c) the amount to be found in houses where the householder is willing to receive unaccompanied children or teachers.

The Minister believes that this is a matter which can only be effectively carried out through the machinery of Local Government, and he has been glad to learn from the discussions he has had with representatives of the Associations of Local Authorities and teachers that he can rely on their cordial co-operation.

The Minister requests that the authority will take steps to put this survey in hand without delay, and he knows that all authorities can be relied upon to appreciate the importance of carrying it out with expedition and with tact. It will be necessary to appoint a number of visitors to act under the direction of the Chief Officer to conduct the survey. The selection of visitors is a matter for the authority, but it appears to the Minister that the best results are likely to be obtained by a judicious combination of skilled official personnel and of voluntary efforts.

The Minister will be glad to receive a return on the enclosed (form E V 4) not later than 28th February 1939.

After a general discussion on the above Circular, and after perusal of the enclosures, it was recommended

a) that the Clerk be appointed as the Council's Executive Officer,
b) that the Chairman issue a letter to every householder in the area, model on Form B,
c) the Clerk write to members of the Council together with Womens' Institutes and other public bodies with a view to obtaining names and addresses of possible suitable volunteers,
d) the Financial Officer arrange with Mr. R. P. Willis to assist Mr. F. Bell with his collections with a view to relieving him for office duties.

28th JANUARY 1939 (D/S)
National Service in the North Riding.

Lord Bolton pointed out that the Government had decided that the National Service campaign should be on a voluntary basis and, whether as individuals they agreed with the decision or not, it was definitely the duty of the committee (National Service) to use every endeavour to make it a success. The three main functions of the committee were, first, to stimulate recruitment for the various offices of national service enumerated in the

National Service Guide which would be issued to all householders in the near future; secondly, to co-ordinate recruitment for these services in such a way as to avoid the overcrowding of one service at the expense of another; and to set up, under the aegis of the committee, interviewing panels to be attached to each of the Ministry of Labour National Service Offices in the county.

4th FEBRUARY 1939 (D/S)
Bomb Shelters Tested.
There will be general satisfaction at the results of the tests applied at Shoeburyness to the portable steel air raid shelters which the Government is having made in large quantities for free distribution in poor districts. A heavy bomb was sunk 18 inches in the ground near some cottages and two shelters and detonated. When the explosion was over the cottages had disappeared but the shelters, only ten yards off, were unaffected , either by the blast or by the shower of bricks and timber. The heavy steel plates would, it is clear, have protected people inside the shelters from the concussion or from the flying splinters.

Safety Camps for Children
The development of the Government scheme for the establishment of hut camps for civilians from crowded areas exposed to air raids in time of war will be watched with interest. To begin with fifty such camps, each accommodating 350 persons, will be built at a total cost of a million pounds.

11th MARCH 1939 (D/S)
Suggestion for Thirsk Rural District Council.
Sir, - If, as stated by 'North Riding Farmer', farmers will, for several months, have virtually no time to spare, one wonders why Thirsk Rural District Council, which is largely composed of farmers, do not hold meetings in the evening, when presumably time is a less vital factor, instead of during the day. Perhaps they would have more time to go into the question of trade facilities for the beautiful, but badly lit town of Thirsk.

Since pleasure and entertainment play an important role in the trade of a town, I suggest that the Sutton Bank hill climb be revised, but on a rough road constructed off the main road up the hillside, and that more facilities be given for recreation and games, especially tennis. There is not one hard court available for the public.

There should not be any question about employment at the aerodromes if money could only be granted to undertake the work which urgently requires doing, such as an efficient sewerage scheme, making good the housing shortage, bus shelters, A. R. P. work and improvements to the market place.

If these schemes were undertaken not only would our own unemployed be found work, but those from a wide area.

Sowerby, Thirsk March 6th 1939. Danum.

25th March 1939 (D/S)
Volunteers For Thirsk Territorials.

At a meeting of the North Riding National Service Committee it was stated that at Thirsk the local command of the Territorials was up to establishment and that a number of eligible recruits were available but could not be accepted. A suggestion was made that a reserve list should be prepared so that as vacancies arose recruits could be used to replace these. It was decided that the matter should be brought before the North Riding Territorial Association.

It was further said that volunteers were still required for Auxiliary Fire Services and R.A.F. at Thirsk.

27th March 1939 (T.R.D.C.)
Housing Provision.

The Finance Committee considered the following letter from the Air Ministry in regard to the provision of houses for personnel at Dishforth Aerodrome. After general discussion on the matter it was resolved that this Council do nothing in this matter.

8th April 1939 (D/S)
MUSSOLINI STRIKES IN ALBANIA.

Italian troops land at four points.

The official British view is that conflicting reports made it difficult to get an authoritative picture of what has happened.

24th April 1939 (T.R.D.C.)
Correspondence.

Circular letter from the Home Office requesting the Local Authority so to arrange their business that during the next three months priority be given to Civil Defence matters over other business before the Authority.

Letter from the Lt. Colonel, Commanding 4th Battalion, The Green Howards, asking the Council to enlist their active and vigorous co-operation and assistance in raising recruits.

1st May 1939. (T.R.D.C.)
Emergency Fire Brigade in Wartime.

The Financial Officer reported that he had received Form E.F.B.2 for completion to this Council's application for Emergency Fire Brigade Equipment

8th May 1939 (T.R.D.C.)
Medical Officer of Health's Report.

The Medical Officer of Health reported generally on the activities in regard to First Aid under Air Raid Precautions. He stated that during the crisis he had made arrangements for twenty-six nursing points in the area and certain equipment had been purchased and although this expenditure would not be recognised by the County as ranking for grant, he was of the opinion that the Council should reimburse the cost of such equipment to the Nursing Association who had purchased same.

Recommended that these amounts be paid on receipt of satisfactory invoices.

The Medical Officer also reported, in regard to training of First Aid Parties, there would be the cost of Gas training which does not rank as expenditure for grant.

Recommended that the Council pay such additional cost.

Correspondence.

Letter from the North Eastern Electric Supply Co. enclosing copy proposals to supply certain Parishes in the area with electricity.

Letter from the R.A.S.C. in regard to the cleaning of latrines which would be necessary for Territorial Army Camp at Thirsk.

The Sanitary Inspector reported on correspondence he had had with the R.A.S.C. (Royal Army Service Corp.)

Recommended that the latrines be cleaned at the minimum charge of 17/6 per journey if the camp is situated within one mile of the town.

27th May 1939 (D/S)
'We Love The Peace' says German youth.
Letter to a Harrogate Headmaster.

Addressing Thirsk Rotarians at their weekly luncheon at the Fleece Hotel, Thirsk, on Thursday on the international situation, Mr. J.T. Lancaster, B.A., M. Litt, Headmaster of Ashville College, Harrogate, read a letter from a German youth, received following a decision to cancel a visit of the school hockey team to Germany owing to the European situation.

The letter read, 'I was very astonished that the English people think so much of war. When your letter arrived it was first of May, the Day of Peace in Germany and all Germans were glad and gay. We love the peace! Why do you think, in England, we should like to begin war. Do you think we want to work hard in our country for the bombardment of your aeroplanes? No, never!

But you mustn't think that we wish to expose all our work without fight. Therefore we have a great army now. We are full of trust for our Fuhrer and no man and no wife thinks of war.

Now you see that you could have come to Germany without fear. We laughed at the sentence 'on account of the political situation we didn't come. Besides I was very glad of the words 'I love Germany, and the very many good friends I have made in different parts of your country.

I hope you will tell your friends and other people in England that they need not fear war.'

Biggest Danger.

Mr. Lancaster said it was amazing how many Germans, including intelligent people, knew so little of such matters. The biggest danger was that the German people had no conception of how near to war they were last September.

Dealing with other matters concerning the European situation, Mr. Lancaster said he was sure Britains now had right-thinking Americans behind them. America was nearer them today than she had ever been. The stock of the doctrine of might has gone down considerably in the last six months, he went on, and all the medieval savagery in other countries has horrified the rest of the civilised world.

There is now a more powerful alignment against those powers than ever before, and democracy, with all it stands for, has never been higher.

The Rev. G.D. John, (Vicar of Sowerby), who proposed a vote of thanks to the speaker, recounted a conversation with a refugee who said it was most difficult for anybody who did not see Hitler's point of view to live in Germany.

27th MAY 1939 (D/S)
Empire Air Day. Bombers and Fighters in Dishforth Display.

A crowd estimated between sixteen and seventeen thousand saw the R.A.F. display its power at Dishforth Aerodrome where the attendance reached such proportions that a car park on one side of the airfield was extended to a quarter of a mile in length with cars closely packed five deep.

Visitors came on cycle and foot from the surrounding districts, and from further afield in parties by car and bus. One hangar was cleared of planes and equipped as a catering centre, and here the N.A.A.F.I. were kept busy throughout the afternoon serving tea to thousands of people.

Loudspeakers placed at vantage points on the aerodrome boomed forth a running commentary on the show, as an observer, standing high above the crowds on the control tower kept them informed of what was going on.

Occasionally, there was the rapid fire of machine guns from the men at target practice on a nearby shooting range, while crowds walked in a stream through No.2 hangar, where a gallery had been erected around a Whitley bomber for close inspection. Air cameras and photographs of the surrounding countryside, bombs, guns and pistols; a display of flight equipment such as night flying beacons and floodlights, navigation and radio equipment were also on show, along with a suspended parachute, with the harness attached to a dummy.

Numbers 78 and 10 (Bomber) Squadrons, whose machines took part in the display at Dishforth, moved to the station on its completion in 1937.

9th June 1939 (T.R.D.C.)
Fire Engine.
The Financial Officer submitted quotations he had received in regard to the conversion of the fire engine from solid tyres to pneumatic tyres.

24th June 1939 (D/S)
A Test of Britain's Patience.
Sir, - That the British people are a patient people, has now become proverbial, but is there not such a thing as stretching even elastic to breaking point? And the question is, how much further may things go with us, before that point is reached.

Germany, Italy and Japan have each of them had a twist of the Lion's tail, and even little Ireland has now had a share in the fun. Can the attitude of Mr. Chamberlain be regarded as that of a responsible British statesman? He has talked while other peoples have been doing, until now they interpret his talk as evidence of weakness.

If Disraeli or Gladstone had been with us today the accounts of Germany and Italy would have been settled long ago. Surely it is time Mr. Chamberlain retired and handed the reins of government to younger and more capable hands. We are reaping the fruit of the seed we have been sowing for the last few years, and if we continue so to sow, what will the harvest be?

Yours etc. W. T. Porter.

KILBURN FEAST SPORTS.
MONDAY, July 10th
OPEN LEAPING CONTEST.
PONY LEAPING CONTEST.
Also many other Events.
For particulars apply J. KIRK (Sec.),
Kilburn, York.

15th July 1939 (D/S)
Notes of the Week.
Danzig continues to be the centre of international unrest, but after the Prime Minister's statement in the House of Commons there is no room for doubt about the attitude of Great Britain. Any attempt by Germany to seize Danzig by force or fraud will find us supporting Poland, though if Herr Hitler cares to negotiate for fresh arrangements with 'peaceful intentions and peaceful methods of procedure' Poland will be ready for conversation.

Be Prepared.
A leaflet issued to householders this week may be commended for its conciseness. It is 'Public Information leaflet No. 1' and if subsequent issues are as forceful and informative, the Government department responsible will deserve the thanks of all who receive them. Most official documents are

difficult to understand, but in this instance someone with a flair for directness has shown how it is possible to convey in comparatively few words a good deal of practical information.

The signals to be given as air raid warnings are tersely described, and there are hints on the use of gas masks, emphatic warnings as to lighting restrictions, the precautions to be taken against the effects of incendiary bombs, arrangements for the evacuation of children from danger zones, and clear cut advice that the storage of non-perishable goods before an emergency arises is a form of national service. There is also a wise suggestion that 'if war should come' everybody should carry a label - not a mere scrap of paper - on which is written the name and address of the bearer.

The issue of this pamphlet should disarm the many critics of air raid precautions, and if the leaflets to be issued later are in the same strain there should be no excuse for anyone being in ignorance of what to do in the event of happenings which we all hope will be avoided.

29th July 1939 (D/S)

Fine weather favours Thirsk Show

Good attendance despite call of hay harvest.

The steady progress of Thirsk Show over the past years from the time when it was threatened with extinction owing to agricultural depression, is considered a remarkable achievement in North Riding farming circles.

Thirsk Agricultural Society's decision to carry on with a wider appeal with show and gala at a time when some Yorkshire shows are winding up their affairs, was something of a gamble, for the industry was in a parlous state, but the step was justified and there was ample proof of this at the annual show on Wednesday at the Old Show Ground, Sutton Road. The day was perhaps one on which good weather was a doubtful blessing. After days of rain many farmers would naturally take advantage of fine weather to get in their belated hay harvest and the attendance at the show would

THIRSK AND DISTRICT AGRICUL-
TURAL SOCIETY.

President:
MISS M. FURNESS, M.P.H.

THE ANNUAL SHOW
Will be held on the Old Show Ground,
YORK ROAD, THIRSK
(Entrance Sutton Road). on
WEDNESDAY, July 26th, 1939.
Judging commences 12.30 p.m.
Classes for Hunters, Agricultural Horses, Cattle, Sheep, Pigs, Goats, Honey, Bread, Farm Produce, Garden Produce, Flowers, Etc.
A DOG SHOW will be held under the auspices of the Thirsk and Northaller-ton District Canine Society. Under Kennel Club Rules. Judging commences at 3.30 p.m.
LEAPING—Open to all England After-noon and Evening.
Thirsk and Sowerby Prize Silver Band. will play selections during the day.
GRAND EVENING PROGRAMME.
"The VANTIS TRIO" in "Western Pastimes, featuring Rope-Spinning, Lasso and Whip Manipulation.
"CODA," The Continental Wire-walker.
"THE FOUR CRANKS" Comedy Acro-batic Tumblers in "Springing sur-prises.
"ARBELL," in Aerial Thrills on the Swinging Trapeze, assisted by "Gloria."
The Thirsk Coronation Prize Harmonica Band.
CLAY PIGEON SHOOT, 6.30 p.m.
Teas and Refreshments at reasonable prices available on the Ground.
Admission: Adults Day Ticket 1/6, after 5.30 p.m. 1/-, including Tax. Children's Day Ticket, 1/-, after 5.0 p.m. 6d.
For Schedules, etc., apply B. LANE FOX, F.A.I., Secretary, 2, Kirkgate, Thirsk.

consequently be affected. As it happened the sun shone brilliantly throughout the day and although in the early afternoon the attendance was sparse, the early evening and night attendance was up to expectations....

Throughout the afternoon and evening there were selections by the Thirsk and Sowerby Prize Band, conducted by Mr R Reast. Later, there was also music by the Thirsk Harmonic Band, conducted by Mr A Swift, the evening programme concluding with a dance in the marquee to music by Mr H Knowlson's 'Night Birds' Orchestra.

31st July 1939 (T.R.D.C.)

The Chairman, (Mr. Lomas), read a letter from the Air Raid Precautions Officer stating that, in the event of war, it was certain that he would be called away immediately and he asked the committee whether they wished him to carry on as Hon. Air Raid Precautions Officer or appoint someone who would be present in time of war.

After general discussion on the matter, it was agreed that Colonel Littleboy continues as the Hon. Air Raid Precautions Officer and Mr. Broadway, his deputy, agreed to carry on the Colonel's duties until such time as further arrangements were made.

The question of storing perishable goods in Thirsk was raised.

14th August 1939 (T.R.D.C.)
Government Evacuation Scheme.

The Chairman reported that he had perused Circular 1841 from the Ministry of Health.

Recommended.

That the Committee agree to submit to the Chairman the list of Billeting Officers as set forth in the printed copy of the Evacuation Scheme, as Billeting Officers for appointment.

That a list of names be drawn up from which tribunals can be elected and that two ladies be selected from the list of organisers shown in the printed documents.

That Mr. E. Reed be appointed as Chief Billeting Officer and Mr. White to act as his deputy.

28th August 1939 (T.R.D.C.)
Correspondence.

Letter and plan from the North Eastern Electric Supply Co.Ltd. intimating their intention of erecting overhead electricity lines to the housing estate on Sutton Road, Thirsk.

Recommended that the Council communicate with the Electric Supply Co. insisting that the lines be laid underground.

Letter from the Army Recruiting Officer to the Chairman, giving notice of the attendance of the Band of the 1st Battalion, The Green Howards, on 30thSeptember 1939.

Wireless Programme for Today.

THE B.B.C. announces that news bulletins will be broadcast at the following hours only: 8 a.m., 12 noon, 4 p.m., 6 p.m., 9 p.m., and 12 midnight. Fresh items of important news will continue to be placed as far as possible at the beginning of each bulletin. News of urgent importance received between the regular news bulletins will continue to be treated as at present—that is if received during programme hours it will be broadcast at the hour and if received between midnight and 7 a.m. it will be broadcast at 1 a.m., 3 a.m. or 5 a.m. only.

Official and other public announcements as distinct from news will continue to be broadcast at 7.30 p.m. and 10.30 p.m.

Subject to last-minute alterations, the B.B.C. will broadcast the following programmes:-

TO-DAY.

7.0 a.m.—Time; News.

7.10—Records: Bournemouth Municipal Orchestra; Eide Norena (soprano); Alfred Campoli (violin); Drury Lane Theatre Orchestra; Marcel Moyse (flute); Alfred Cortot (piano); Peter Dawson (bass-baritone); Grand Opera Orchestra.

8.0—Time, News.

8.10—The Carlton Trio.

8.30—Records: Ignaz Friedman (piano); Dennis Noble (baritone); Kreisler (violin).

9.0—B.B.C. Northern Orchestra.

10.0—Records: William Brownlow (baritone).

10.15—The Daily Service.

10.30—Sandy Macpherson at the B.B.C. Theatre Organ.

11.0—Recital: Berkeley Mason (piano); Douglas Cameron (cello).

11.30—Records: B.B.C. Military Band.

12.0—Time; News.

12.15—B.B.C. Salon Orchestra.

12.45—Away From It All: Readings from literature having nothing whatever to do with current affairs.

1.0—Time; News.

1.15—B.B.C. Orchestra.

2.0—Sandy Macpherson at the organ.

2.15—Records: Charles Ancliffe and his Orchestra; Nan Maryska (soprano); Dennis Noble and Orchestra; B.B.C. Wireless Chorus; Heddle Nash and Orchestra; Parry Jones' (tenor); B.B.C. Military Band.

3.0—B.B.C. Scottish Orchestra.

4.0—Time. News.

4.15—Take Your Choice: A Thirty-Minute Mixture; with Gwen Lewis, Horace Percival, Margaret Eaves, Sidney Burchall, Leonard Henry, the Three Chimes; B.B.C. Variety Orchestra.

4.45—Records: Alfred Cortot (piano).

5.0—Children's Hour.

5.30—Movie Melodies: Selection of Songs you remember from the films you saw; sung by Betty Huntley-Wright, Webster Booth, Diana Clare, Sam Costa, B.B.C. Revue Chorus; B.B.C. Variety Orchestra.

6.0—Time; News.

6.15—London and Scottish Announcements.

6.25—The Amateur Handyman in Wartime, by W. P. Matthew.

6.45—Flute Recital by Arthur Gleghorn.

7.0—Welsh and Western Announcements.

7.10—Men of Action: Comedy; with Cecil Trouncer, Leslie Perrins, Philip Wade, Norman Shelley.

7.30—Announcements.

7.45—Northern Announcements.

7.55—Interval.

8.0—The White Coons: A Concert Party Show; with Tommy Handley, C. Denier Warren, Wynne Ajello, Dudley Rolph, Vera Lennox; Harry S. Pepper and Doris Arnold (pianos).

9.0—Time, News.

9.15—To-night's Talk: A series of Talks on important topics of the day.

9.30—B.B.C. Theatre Orchestra.

10.0—Religious Service.

10.20—Records: Myra Hess (piano); Frank Merrick (piano).

10.30—Announcements.

10.45—Midland and Northern Ireland Announcements.

10.55—Interval.

11.0—Triumph Over Time: Poems.

11.15—Dance Music (records).

12.0-12.15—Time; News.

Recommended that the Council give the Army Recruiting Office every assistance.

The Clerk (Mr. F.Stockton-Gowland), reported that, owing to the present emergency, it had been necessary to cancel holidays.

Telephone extensions.

It was reported that, during the crisis, the Clerk's Office had been open day and night, but to obviate the necessity of this, it had been arranged to install extensions to the Financial Officer's, (Mr. W.A.Wilkinson), house in Stockton Road and the Sanitary Inspector's (Mr. F.Metcalfe) house in Green Lane East.

Recommended that the arrangement be approved.

2ᵗʰ SEPTEMBER 1939 (D/S)

North Riding Ready for Air Raids.

After months of planning and scheming the North Riding now has an A.R.P. organisation almost perfect. For administrative purposes, the Riding is divided into two areas. There are 130 First Aid parties, of which 60 are in Number 1 area and 70 in Number 2 area.

Thirsk Rural District Council has allocated The Lambert Memorial Hospital as a First Aid post.

GERMAN INVASION OF POLAND

Prime Minister's Solemn Words to Nation. 'We Are Ready.'

Herr Adolf Hitler, leader of the German nation, yesterday ordered a full scale offensive along the whole of the Polish Corridor.

Evacuation Scenes In The North East.

700 Gateshead children at Thirsk.

More than 700 children from Gatshead were billeted in Thirsk, Sowerby and surrounding villages yesterday. They arrived in two trainloads and were taken to Thirsk Racecourse, where they were given hot drinks and sandwiches. Later they were taken to their new homes.

The billeting scheme was carried out by Mr. G.R.White, Thirsk Housing Inspector, helped by Mr. E.Reed, (Chief Billeting Officer) and volunteers. Thirsk has 104 evacuees and the remainder are in the villages. A similar number of evacuees from Gateshead is expected today.

CHAPTER TWO
September 1939 to December 1939

3rd SEPTEMBER 1939

WAR DECLARED

Prime Minister Neville Chamberlain spoke on the wireless from the Cabinet Room at 10, Downing Street, 'This morning the British Ambassador in Berlin handed the Germans a final note stating that, unless we heard from them by eleven o'clock that they were prepared at once to withdraw their troops from Poland, a state of war would exist between us. I have to tell you that no such undertaking has been received and that subsequently this country is at war with Germany. Now may God bless you all. May he defend the right. It is the evil things we shall be fighting against - brute force, bad faith, injustice, oppression and persecution - and against them I am certain that right will prevail.'

AND THE WAR CAME.

Ann Coates. *A child at the time at Kilburn.*

'A first memory of war that touched the school was when we all went to Mrs. Hugill's house after school. We were taken into one of her rooms that was piled high with gas masks. As soon as she had fitted us with one we took it home and carried it to school each day. I was one of the last to be fitted and arrived home quite late to find a frantic mother worried to death about where I had been.

Shortly after this we all had to walk to Coxwold and just along the Byland Road to the village hall. There was a 'gas van' there and we all had to go inside and stay there with our masks on to make sure they were all working. We went in small groups and it took a while.

Suddenly the village was full of children and quite a lot of mothers. The evacuees had arrived. We didn't get any on the farm as we were considered too far from the village. The Big Classroom had a hessian curtain fitted to make another little area for a third class and a man teacher. Quite a novelty. Some mothers and children did not stay long and headed for home.

Word spread round the village. Some evacuee mothers had gone into the pub for a drink. Women did NOT go into pubs. The landlord, George Bolton, was a great character. My brother and a couple of friends

L·N·E·R EXCURSIONS

(From Monday, 4th, to Saturday, 9th Sept., incl.)

CANCELLATION OF EXCURSION BOOKINGS

The Railway Company regret that in consequence of the evacuation of the civil population they have been reluctantly compelled to cancel all excursion bookings on Saturday, 2nd September, and Sunday, 3rd September. A further announcement will be made in Saturday's local Press respecting the running of the under-mentioned excursions.

were cycling through the village and decided to have a drink, to be met with 'Thoo lot int ord eneeuf.' He then served them. (This was several years later)

3rd SEPTEMBER 1939

National Service (Armed Forces) Act came into being. All Men Between 18 and 41 Years of Age Liable For Conscription.

4th SEPTEMBER 1939 (T.R.D.C).

The Clerk reported that he had received instructions from the Food (Defence Plans) Department, to set up a Food Control Committee to consist of fifteen members of whom not less than five will be trade members including,

a) a retail grocer or provision merchant.
b) a retail butcher or flesher.
c) an officer of a retail Co-operative Society.
d) two representatives of other food outlets.

9th SEPTEMBER 1939 (D/S)

Evacuees in North Riding Village.
Pathos and Humour of a New Life.

Tragic though war is, there is, outside of its casualties, a pathos and humour to be found in the comradeship and fine feelings of the mothers and evacuee children from Gateshead, as well as in the fighting forces of our nation. Here are a few examples from first hand.

By the **Rev. E.J.Collins** (*Carlton Miniott*)

A mother came into the Paying Officer at one of our local villages. She is sturdy, and in her arms are two bonny babies.

'You must come tomorrow for your money,' says the officer.

'How can I come, carrying these two?' retorts the mother, 'and I have two other young children at another village, and can't get to them.' I have walked four miles here with this load. You must help me or I will collect up my bairns and make for home.'

Moved with compassion, a young lady assistant paying out officer offered to nurse one of the children while the mother was called upon to sign the necessary Ministry form.

PETROL RATIONING SCALE.

FOUR GALLONS A MONTH MINIMUM ALLOWANCE.

Following is the scale of units when petrol rationing comes into force on September 16th—the unit for the present being one gallon:—

Cars up to seven horse-power, four units a month.

Eight to nine h.p. five units.

Ten to 12 h.p., six units.

Thirteen to 15 h.p., seven units.

Sixteen to 19 h.p., eight units.

Twenty h.p. and over, 10 units.

Motor-cycles, two units.

It has been calculated that the rationing according to horse-power will allow an average of 150 miles a month, but it is probable that the owners of cars from eight to nine horse-power will achieve nearer 200 miles a month with their allowance of five gallons of petrol. Even cars with a horse-power greater than 20 do surprisingly high mileages per gallon if rapid acceleration is not sought, and it may well be that on the allowances the average motorist will be able to cover 50 miles per week.

Motorists will have to apply for ration books with their registration books either personally at the post office where they usually obtain their car licences or at the local taxation office, or by post at the latter.

The price will be 1s 6d a gallon.

The offer being accepted, the mother, seizing the other child, says,' I'll write with this,' holding the second child out like a huge fountain pen, covered with a Michelin tyre.

A smile came when the money was paid and she trudged off happily four miles, carrying 80 lbs on her hips, to her temporary home, as bravely as any soldier - indeed her husband had been called up as a reservist.

Olga Brown, *(nee Dickinson)*.

When I became an evacuee from Gateshead I was taken to a small village called Thornton-le-Moor, Yorkshire. It was dark when we arrived and we went

SAVE NEWSPAPERS TO MAKE NEW PAPER

into a hall. We were being chosen for the place we would be living at. My two brothers were with me, their names were read out and off they went. I was left all on my own as somebody had left my name off the list. I was taken to a cottage where I stayed for two months.

The second house I did not like. They were a well-off family. When I came home from school I had to go to the kitchen where cook gave me a glass of milk, a slice of bread and butter then I had to go to bed. I wasn't allowed to play out. The family had a boy and a girl but I only saw them twice in six months. I was told one Saturday they were going off in their car. Do not touch the bikes - play with the old one. I was very happy when they told me they were moving away.

All change again. This time an older lady living alone took me in. I hated mornings. Before I could have breakfast I had to go to a farm up the road for milk. They had a billy goat tied up outside the big gates. I used to talk to it, 'Billy, I'm scared to go in for the geese are in the farmyard.' I used to run across that farmyard as they used to run after me and peck my legs. I said one day that I wasn't going back, I would go to the other farm where my brother was. That worked, for the farmer started bringing the milk down.

School was good. We went for walks along the country lanes. I adored these walks. The teacher was good. Twice she took three in her car so we could visit our parents for the week-end. Also another teacher took a brother and sister home. Sadly a bomb dropped on their home and they were both killed.

I loved it when Saturday and Sunday came. Sometimes when I went up to the farm I was shown how to fill milk bottles up then put the tops on. I put the bottles in the crate ready for the farmer to take to his customers. I hated having to leave the farm and go back up to the house where I was staying. It was very lonely. Mrs. Hurd would not let me touch anything. I once asked her if she would teach me to play the piano but it was, 'No, and don't try and open it as it is locked.'

My second Christmas there I never forgot. Before the war I loved Christmas. All my aunts brought me presents and my grandparents always came with presents. I always hung a pillow case up and a long stocking and there were always games placed on the table. Yes, I missed all that. In the summer when mam came she would bring me things like comics and books. Once she brought me new shoes. I loved them. They were cream coloured like the colour of biscuits. They had a strap going across which fastened on to a button. I felt real posh. But within one week my happiness was gone. Where were my lovely new shoes? They had been taken from me and given to Mrs. Hurd's niece and I was given her old black ones. I cried for hours. I knew I had to do something. My mother always made me keep one shilling hidden in case she was needed and I had to send a post card. I took a pencil and went to the Post Office, bought a card and a stamp, sat outside on the grass and wrote to my mother saying that my new shoes had been given away. Then I pushed the post card into the letter box. I went to see Mrs. Hutchinson and told her what I had done.

Next week my mother came and demanded that the shoes be back in half an hour. She also said that she wanted an explanation then added that she was taking me home. I ran and got my clothes and other things. Was I happy? The shoes came back and when my mam asked why they had been taken she was told they were hurting me. Mother certainly told her off.

WHAT TO DO IN AN AIR RAID : MEMORISE THESE POINTS.

Government announcements affecting the life of the civil population in wartime were issued by the Lord Privy Seal on Sunday. They include procedure to be followed during air raids.

AIR RAID WARNINGS.

In the event of threatened air raids warnings will be given in urban areas by means of sirens or hooters, which will be sounded in some places by short intermittent blasts and in other places by a warbling note changing every few seconds. The warning may also be given by short blasts on police whistles. No hooter or siren may be sounded except on the instructions of the police.

When you hear any of these sounds—take shelter.

Do not leave your shelter until you hear the " Raiders passed " signal, which will be given by continuously sounding the sirens or hooters for a period of two minutes on the same note.

If poison gas has been used you will be warned by means of hand rattles. If you hear hand rattles do not leave your shelter until the poison gas has been cleared away. Hand bells will be used to tell you when there is no longer any danger from poison gas.

GENERAL.

Keep off the streets as much as possible. To expose yourself unnecessarily adds to your danger.

Carry your gas masks with you always.

Make sure that you and every member of your household, especially children able to run about, have on them their names and addresses clearly written. Do this either on an envelope or something like a luggage label, not on a piece of paper which might get lost. Sew the label on to your children's clothes where they cannot pull it off.

[Cut this out. Paste it on a card. You will need it at least until you have memorised it.]

We went down to the farm to say goodbye to Mr. and Mrs. Hutchinson and my brother Bobby, also my other brother Reg. In two and a half years I only saw him twice. At home I was so afraid when the sirens started up. We did not have a shelter but mam had white-washed the cupboard out under the stairs. She put a mattress in, torches, candles, matches, blankets and pillows. Every night she made cocoa and filled a thermos flask. You can bet we would get to sleep, then the sirens would go. One Monday teatime we had just sat down to tea when there was an awful big bang - our windows shook. I dived under the table. Yes, a bomb had gone off down Gateshead High Street. We went down later to look. A shelter had been hit but as there had not been any air raid siren it was empty.

1943 was a very sad year. My father took ill and died. A few months later Grandad and Grandmother moved to Monkwearmouth where they were publicans. Me and mam went to see them for tea one day and they gave me money for ice-cream. I didn't know it would be the last time I would see him. He died the next week, killed by a bomb explosion. Mam did not tell me for a long time afterwards.

We, the children of the war years had to grow up quick. We had to learn a lot about life. Should I have come home from Yorkshire ? Yes, after all I had my family who were loving and caring and that is what I wanted.

16th September 1939 (D/S)
Unauthorised Sounding Of Hooters Banned

The Ministry of Information announced on Thursday that an order has been issued under the Defence Regulations forbidding anyone to sound within public hearing any siren, hooter, whistle, rattle, bell, horn, gong or similar instrument, except in accordance with the directions for air raid warning purpose.

The firing of maroons and other fireworks fired from a mortar is prohibited. The order does not affect railwaymen or ships' crews. Police whistles, fire alarm bells, church bells or normal use of bicycle bells and motor horns are not affected.

Dr. May Wyon. *Resident of Thirsk.*

Dr. May Wyon was married to a fellow doctor some four days after war broke out in 1939. Peter, her husband, was Dr. MacArthur's assistant, and after a brief honeymoon in the Lake District the newlyweds settled into a cottage in Victoria Avenue, Thirsk.

In 1940 Dr. Peter Wyon joined the Royal Army Medical Corps and was to see service in Madagascar, South Africa, India and Burma. It would be some years before the couple were reunited.

May's memories of life in Thirsk during the early part of the war are vivid. She recalls the long hours worked by her husband, the manning of the telephone, the making of pills and the mixing of medicines. The poor sanitation, and the lack of good, clean water in a number of cottages, not only in Thirsk but also in the villages, contributed to a number of outbreaks of disease. The tin sheeted Fever Hospital, off Sutton Road, was well used for those with scarlet fever, diphtheria and other infectious diseases. Patients were sent there to isolate them from the community in an attempt to stop the disease spreading. Very strict visiting hours were enforced under the watchful eye of the matron and special fever transport was also used. It was a stressful time, not only for patients but also for relatives.

Norby had its fair share of poor housing. The rooms were tiny, generally one up and one down for a husband and wife with five or six children. Often there was no inside tap and middens were the norm. The neglected structure of the cottages left much to be desired but May Wyon remembers the people who lived in such poor housing as generally very happy who did their best for their children.

The Lambert Memorial Hospital was well used. In the early years of the war it had its own operating theatre where minor operations were carried out. One of the oddities of the theatre was the presence of a coal fire. One of the carers at the hospital, Mrs. Denham, was, in May's opinion, 'a wonderful carer'.

May used to swap her sweet coupons for clothes coupons and recalls the plane crash on Hood Hill where a very large rock was shattered when the plane hit it. She remembers the delivery of coal to the cottages and houses by horse and cart and the barometer on the Post Office which indicated how well the town was performing in raising money for the war effort. Once her husband had left for the army she returned to her parents in Leeds to await his return.

Dave Brown. *Resident of Thirsk.*

When war was declared against Germany in 1939 Dave was staying with his grandfather in Redcar. On coming home he was not sure what to expect for like so many of his pals he had seen the results of the bombing in the Spanish Civil War on the newsreels at the cinema.

At the start of the war the children were issued with gas masks in a cardboard box. The box had a string through so that you could put it over your shoulder. Then a canvas bag was bought to put the box in. 'After we got our gas masks we went down to the Infant School in Finkle Street where they had a wagon like a furniture van. We went into the van wearing our gas masks and were asked if we could smell anything. We were O.K. and they said, 'take the mask off and smell the gas then put the mask back on', and we went out. That was so we would know what it smelt like.

Sometimes we did lessons with our gas masks on (can still smell the rubber). We used to cheat by putting something in the side to let more air in.

It was not long before the gas mask was left out of its box and other things such as sweets and apples carried. We did not carry our gas mask all through the war, only about a couple of years.'

At the age of eleven Dave entered the Church of England School in Piper Lane, Thirsk. A Woodwork and Cookery centre was also available for the pupils in Picks Lane. Woodwork pupils had to bring their own wood due to wartime restrictions. Metalwork was also taught. As there were plenty of bullets about the boys used to make cigarette lighters from them. Gardening was yet another subject introduced at the Church School. Here the pupils were taught to 'Dig For Victory!'

Dave recalls a heap of Molotov cocktails piled up in case of invasion. Dave and John Swift used to test the stirrup pump (used to put out small fires) on the garden.

During Dave's last year at school, to help with the harvest, pupils could get a permit for twenty half days to work on farms. The farmer could also apply for a further permit. Dave and his pal used to work hoeing sugar beet and turnips. The boys also used to help with spreading muck from the farm carts on to the fields.

Dave joined the Air Scouts in 1941. They met at the Secondary School under the leadership of Eric Lee. Plane recognition, drill, navigation and Morse signalling were some of the skills learned. Part of Dave's war effort was the collection of salvage. The Scouts had a hand cart and this was used to collect glass and waste paper. These were taken to a garage in The White Swan yard. The gathering of rose hips to make Rose-hip syrup (rich in Vitamin C) was also encouraged. One of the highlights of the Air Training Corps was a plane trip from Leeming when they flew seven times round Thirsk. Two sounds Dave will always associate with the war are the sound of the air raid siren and the sound of planes.

One Sunday the Home Guard and the Army put on a display. The Home Guard would defend the Post Office while the Army was supposed to be parachutists who had dropped on the Flatts and attacked the town through the snickets from Chapel Street. A police car with a loudspeaker was giving a commentary to the crowd which were on the Golden Fleece side of the Market Place. The Home Guard set off a drum which was supposed to be smoke near the shops opposite the bull ring. The brown smoke came drifting over the Market Place and people started coughing. Police announced that everything is O.K., it's only smoke but all the crowd got out of the way. Dave went up to the Flatts and laid down near Lock's Bridge. Albert Swift, who was a sergeant in the Home Guard, and someone else, carried the drum up Kirkgate and dropped it in the mill race near the Church. It was said that the drum had been sabotaged making it smoke when it was supposed to be some kind of gas.

11th SEPTEMBER 1939 (T.R.D.C.)
Fuel and Lighting Restrictions Order.

The Clerk reported that he had received instructions to appoint a Local Fuel Officer and to set up a committee to consist of members of the Council and not less than three tradesmen.

15th SEPTEMBER 1939 (T.R.D.C.)
Air Raid Precautions.

The Sanitary Inspector reported that it had been necessary to employ additional labour to fill sand bags as it had been impossible to obtain volunteers to do the work and he asked the Committee to approve payment for this additional labour.

Recommended that this be agreed to.

Maurice Ormston. *Resident of Thirsk.*

Maurice was a member of the congregation at Sessay Church when war was declared. He remembers George Welbourne coming into the church and whispering the news to the vicar who announced it from the pulpit. The majority of those who heard the vicar's words believed the war would be over very soon.

Maurice was not unfamiliar with the threat of war for he had watched the newsreels at the Thirsk cinemas which showed the devastation that could be caused by bombers. He had also seen at first hand some of the Whitley bombers stationed at Dishforth aerodrome. However more pressing events had to be dealt with. The mixed farm his parents had was still completing the harvest. Wheat had to be cut and stooked, stock fed while the horses and carts plied their way to and from the fields.

Shortage of labour became a pressing problem on the farm and it was decided that Maurice should leave Easingwold School to work full-time. Two memories of the early part of the war remain in his memory. One was the arrival of an evacuee at the farm from Gateshead. Maurice's mother was horrified to discover that the lad had nits and lice and got him into a bath. The lad's clothes were taken away and he was kitted out with some of the clothes belonging to the family. The young evacuee's mother was billeted at Knayton and after a few weeks decided to return to Gateshead. 'Mother was not best pleased,' according to Maurice. The other memory is of picking up leaflets which the R.A.F. were dropping over Germany at this time. Many such leaflets were propaganda and tried to assure the ordinary German people that we had no quarrel with them.

As the war progressed the local quarries were re-opened at Carlton Husthwaite. The stone extracted was used by the contractors who were building the airfields at Dalton and Topcliffe. The roads round and through the village became, at times, dangerous places. Once the aerodromes were

BERLINER! Habt Ihr's jetzt begriffen?

Berliner! Habt ihr den Verstand verloren? Wenn sie Euch erzählen, dass jetzt nur noch England allein den Achsenvölkern gegenübersteht, 47 Millionen gegen 200 Millionen, glaubt ihr das? Habt Ihr vergessen, dass es ein britisches Weltreich gibt, in dem 492 Millionen gegen Hitler geeinigt sind? Habt Ihr vergessen, dass von den 200 Millionen Sklaven Hitlers mindestens 80 Millionen besiegte Völker sind, die ihre Unterdrücker hassen und auf ihre Stunde warten; und 44 Millionen sind nur Italiener?! Habt Ihr vergessen, dass die ganze industrielle und landwirtschaftliche Produktion Nord- und Südamerikas gegen Euch mobilisiert wird?

Nein, Berliner, Goebbels sagt nicht immer die Wahrheit. Und wenn er Euch sagt, dass England machtlos, ausgehungert, verängstigt ist und in ein paar Tagen erobert werden wird, glaubt Ihr das auch? Habt Ihr vergessen, dass die britische Kriegsflotte mächtiger ist, als alle übrigen europäischen Flotten zusammen? Habt Ihr unsere Luftwaffe vergessen, die in Deutschland herumfliegt, wie es ihr passt und im Juli allein 37 000 Bomben auf militärische Ziele in der Ruhr und im Rheinland abgeworfen hat! Die Bomben, die mit diesen Flugblättern zusammen abgeworfen wurden, sagen Euch —

der Krieg, den Hitler anfing, geht weiter!

Jawohl, Berliner! Erst einmal müsst ihr nämlich uns besiegen. Und wenn ihr hofft, das durch die Luftblockade schaffen zu können, dann überlegt Euch das lieber zweimal, denn die scheint nicht zu funktionieren. Beinahe ein Jahr lang haben sich Göring und Raeder angestrengt, und unsere Kriegsflotte, unsere Handelsflotte, unsere Luftwaffe und unsere Lebensmittelvorräte in England sind alle viel grösser als im letzten September.

Was nun den Versuch eines Einfalls in England angeht, so glauben wir kaum, dass Hitler dazu dumm genug ist. Grossbritannien ist nicht Norwegen. Der Versuch würde das Ende des Krieges — und das Ende von Hitlers Macht bedeuten.

Nein! Der Krieg wird anders ausgehen. Dieser lange Krieg — der 1933 anfing, denn Krieg ist die einzige Aufgabe der nationalsozialistischen Diktatur — wird nicht aufhören, wenn Hitler es mag. Wann und wie dieser Krieg aufhört, das bestimmen wir — und mit uns die ganze Welt!

Dann Hitler hat sich verrechnet. Auf seine militärische Macht und die Brutalität der Gestapo gestützt, erwartet er, von der Welt, dass sie ihn bewundern soll, den grossen „Eroberer". Aber sie verabscheut ihn. Die nationalsozialistische Diktatur muss untergehen, denn die ganze Aussenwelt ist ihm feindlich, und immer mehr brennt der Hass der Millionen unter seinem Joch.

Volk von Berlin! Früher warst Du einmal als das „hellste" bekannt. Früher wusstet Du, wie Du Deine Meinung durchsetzen konntest. Vielleicht kannst Du nachdenken und herausfinden, wie Du bei Deutschlands Errettung helfen kannst. Im kommenden Kriegswinter aber, und wenn es sein muss noch in vielen Kriegswintern — wirst Du merken, dass wir Recht behalten haben, wenn wir jetzt sagen:

Der Krieg dauert so lange wie Hitlers Regime!

4:4

BERLINERS DO YOU REALISE NOW?

Berliners have you lost your senses? When you tell yourselves that now only England remains opposed to the Axis nations, 47 million against 200 million, do you believe it? Have you forgotten that there is a worldwide British Empire in which 492 million are united against Hitler? Have you forgotten that of the 200 million slaves to Hitler at least 80 million are conquered people who hate their oppressors and wait for their hour to strike; and 44 million are only Italians? I Have you forgotten that the whole of North and South America's industrial and agricultural production is mobilised against you?

No Berliners, Goebbels doesn't always tell the truth. And if he tells you that England is powerless, terrified and will be conquered in a couple of days, do you believe that too? Have you forgotten that the British Navy is more powerful than all the other European navies put together? Have you forgotten our Air Force that flies over Germany at will and in July alone dropped 37,000 bombs at military targets in the Ruhr and Rhineland? The bombs which were dropped with these leaflets tell you --

THE WAR WHICH HITLER BEGAN, CONTINUES !

Yes indeed, Berliners! First you must defeat us. And if you hope to achieve this by an air blockade, then think twice, because it doesn't appear to work. For almost a year Göring and Raeder have striven hard, yet our navy, our merchant navy, our air force and our food supplies in England are all much greater than they were last September.

As to an attempted invasion of England, we scarcely believe that Hitler would be so stupid. Great Britain isn't Norway. The attempt would mean the end of the war - the end of Hitler's might.

No, the war will run a different course. this long war, - which began in 1933, for war is the sole preoccupation of the National Socialist dictatorship - will not end when Hitler wishes.

When and how the war will end will be determined by us and the whole world with us!

For Hitler has miscalculated. Supported by his military might and the brutality of the Gestapo, he expects that the whole world should admire him as the great 'Conqueror'. But it detests him. The National Socialist dictatorship must perish because the whole world is opposed to him and the flames of hatred of those under his oppression blaze ever fiercer.

People of Berlin! You were once known as the most 'clear-headed'. Formerly you knew how to get your own way. Perhaps you can think out how you can best assist in saving Germany.

In the coming winter of war, and if necessary in many winters of war to come, you will be aware that we are right when we now say:

THE WAR WILL LAST AS LONG AS HITLER'S REGIME

Leaflet dropped over Germany (Courtesy of Linton-on-Ouse Memorial Room) active then a number of R.A.F. ground staff used to come for tea and a taste of home life. At Dalton airfield there was a 'battle school' where for a few weeks air crew would be taught about escape techniques should they be shot down. To emphasise the reality of the scheme those on the course would be taken up into the Hambleton Hills and told to evade capture and make their own way back to base. Maurice remembers hiding many an escapee in the farm buildings.

Work on the farm began at 6.30 a.m. with the feeding of the stock followed by breakfast. The men started at seven and at ten an allowance time was taken when cans of tea and home-made scones were provided by the farmer's wife. Dinner was taken between twelve and one and work generally finished at five-thirty. Apart from feeding the stock no farm work was done on Sunday - a tradition still upheld by Maurice. Maurice joined the Home Guard and was issued with a uniform, a rifle and ten bullets. Attendance at drill and training exercises became part of the week's events.

During the early part of the war a searchlight unit was stationed in Sessay. The unit was based in a flimsy wooden hut with the searchlight battery close by. Manned by some sixteen to twenty soldiers this additional feature in the village was yet another talking point about the impact of the war. On change over days the soldiers slept in the school room.

Other events he enjoyed were visits to the cinema in Thirsk where he frequently had to queue to get in. His bike, along with others, would be left in a yard in Finkle Street. Dancing was another pastime he enjoyed. Word of mouth would indicate which village was holding a dance and 'You had to be quick on your feet to get a girl!' Spot prizes were offered of eggs and cakes and now and again an auction would be arranged. The Canadians were generous bidders.

Rationing did not present a problem for the farm had two cows, pigs, poultry and sheep. Rabbits and wood pigeons were also available - the latter would fetch a good price. Maurice remembers the war as a time of improvement in farming, and the friendships made.

25th SEPTEMBER 1939 (T.R.D.C.)
Evacuation Office, Castlegate, Thirsk.

Gentlemen,

I have to report that 1376 evacuees were received as follows:-

1st September	712 school children from Gateshead
2nd September	162 mothers and children.
3rd September	452 school children from Sunderland.
4th September	49 mothers and children.

These were received at Thirsk Railway Station and transported to the Race Course buildings where they were all fed and distributed by buses to the various Parish Distributing Depots and from whence to actual billets. This part of the scheme worked very smoothly and my thanks are due to the various volunteers and Billeting Officers for the excellent way they carried out a very difficult task. Their duties consisted of marshalling, feeding and billeting the evacuees and, in addition, the Billeting Officers had to issue various certificates in respect of each evacuee to the householder.

However it has been reported that a great many complaints have been received in respect of evacuees from Gateshead being in a filthy and verminous condition and many cases of impetigo have been reported. It is not necessary for me to dwell further on this matter as no doubt each individual member will have received a number of complaints. I must say, however, that if these evacuees had been even something approaching clean the work of everybody concerned would have been much easier and most certainly more pleasant.

I should like to ask the Council to take the matter up with the Gateshead Authority with a view to some explanation of the filthy and verminous state of these children which could not have been thoroughly examined by School Medical Authorities to the extent we understand in this district.

Notwithstanding the condition of many of the evacuees the householders have accepted them and done all in their power to eradicate the nuisance, in many cases at great expense and trouble, and I ask the Council to publicly thank these willing householders who have conscientiously met an emergency which even the most pessimistic of us never expected.

Considerable difficulties arose when the mothers arrived on the second day and contrary to any

Thank you, Mrs. Ruggles... we want more like you !

Mrs. Ruggles keeps the little sweet and cigarette shop in the village. She's been looking after her " evacuee " for over six months. Extra work? Yes, Johnnie's been a handful ! . . . . but she knows she has done the right thing.

And think of all the people who have cause to be thanking Mrs. Ruggles. First, young Johnnie himself. He's out of a danger zone—where desperate peril may come at any minute. And he's healthier and happier and better-behaved now. Perhaps he doesn't say it but he certainly means

"Thank you, Mrs. Ruggles". Then his parents. Think what it means to them ! "Whatever happens Johnnie is safe. And with such a dear motherly soul, too. We often say 'Bless you, Mrs. Ruggles'."

. The Government too is grateful to Mrs. Ruggles—and to all the 300,000 others who are looking after evacuated children. But many new volunteers are needed— to share the present burden, and to prepare for any crisis that may come. Won't you be one of them ? You may be saving another Johnnie's life.

The Minister of Health, who has been entrusted by the Government with the conduct of evacuation, asks you urgently to join the Roll of those who are willing to receive children. Please apply to your local Council.

instructions proceeded to move their children, not only from one billet to another but in many cases from one end of the district to another. In addition many mothers evacuated to this area and others who came from Gateshead and Sunderland have taken their children back home entirely against the instructions and in many cases against the children's wishes. This was an unforeseen event and no provision had been made for it, consequently a great deal of extra work both clerical and inspection had been entailed.

Instructions from the Ministry of Health to purchase the requisite blankets and I accordingly obtained 851 blankets and the bill is £412 and I ask the Council to pass same to payment. This amount no doubt seems a large one but we were bound to provide for 2,600 evacuees even though 1,300 arrived.

Now the actual billeting is more or less complete it cannot be assumed that there is no more work to be done, as a matter of fact there will be a great deal of work whilst the evacuees are here, e.g. communal feeding, clothing and other necessary duties for the welfare of the evacuee. The Women's Voluntary Service are undertaking a great deal of this work but the Ministry of Health requires accurate records of the same and this will involve a great deal of clerical work and I suggest the Council should appoint some person to do this work.

I have received a letter from Sunderland stating that they are raising a fund for the provision of boots and clothing for needy cases and they have asked me to submit a list of these and I find these are in the majority, and to carry out distribution of same. I am not aware of any similar scheme for Gateshead evacuees who are greater both in number and need for such a scheme, and I consider it my duty to try and arrange for such a scheme.

In conclusion I wish to thank everyone who has kindly assisted me in the carrying out of this work and for their untiring efforts to make the scheme a success.

Billeting Officer.

25th SEPTEMBER 1939 (T.R.D.C.)
Government Evacuation Scheme.

A detailed report of the Evacuation arrangements was submitted and it was pointed out that Mr. Reed would require assistance, as Mr. White had left the district. It was also pointed out that Mr. Reed and Mr. White had both used their cars unstintingly in carrying out the evacuation arrangements.

Resolved.

That failing to obtain a voluntary assistant the services of a paid assistant be obtained.

a)   That a gratuity of £15.15.0. be awarded to Mr. White.

b)   That an appreciation of Mr. Reed's valuable services be recorded.

Air Raid Precautions.

It was reported that Col. C.N. Littleboy, the Hon. Air Raid Precautions Officer, had been called upon to do Military Service and it was resolved that Mr. A.S.C. Broadway be appointed in his stead.

The question of supplying First Aid Boxes for Air Raid Precautions purposes was raised and it was resolved that the Council pay for all material required in this connection.

13th OCTOBER 1939 (T.R.D.C.)

Recommended that the Post Office be asked to fit warning bells in each fireman's house forthwith.

2nd DECEMBER 1939 (D/S)
RUSSIA'S BRUTAL INVASION OF FINLAND

Repeated aerial attacks on small neighbour.

4th DECEMBER 1939 (T.R.D.C.)
Medical Officer of Health's Report.

The Medical Officer of Health reported that there was an epidemic of diphtheria in the Parishes of Thirsk and Sowerby. He strongly recommended immunisation of children against diphtheria and also reported that he had found it necessary to stop one man working and the Council would be liable to compensate him for loss of wages.

Recommended.

a) That application be made to the Ministry of Health for approval to the immunisation of children against diphtheria.

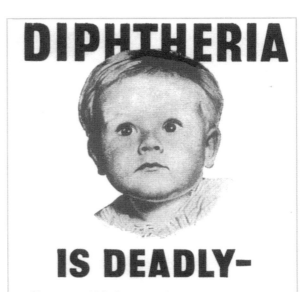

DIPHTHERIA

IS DEADLY–

Give your child the protection medical science now offers. Read the facts below and apply at once to your Council Offices or Welfare Centre—treatment is free.

IMMUNISATION IS THE SAFEGUARD

FACTS ABOUT DIPHTHERIA

Over 50,000 cases occur yearly in Great Britain. Between 2,000 and 3,000 of these die.

Even the best-cared-for child can get Diphtheria—it is not due to dirt or drains—and there are no "safe" areas.

Diphtheria is one of the worst dangers to children. It is particularly deadly to children under six years of age.

Even when not fatal, it may leave ill effects which last a lifetime.

FACTS ABOUT IMMUNISATION

There is nothing to be feared from immunisation. It is SAFE and simple. Merely a "pin prick" which is over and forgotten in a moment. If an immunised child gets Diphtheria it is usually in a mild form. Immunisation gives almost certain protection against death from Diphtheria. Only two treatments are necessary. The best time is soon after the first birthday. Protection takes three months to develop so get your child treated NOW—it is dangerous to delay.

Issued by the Ministry of Health & the Central Council for Health Education

D7a/1

b)   That the Medical Officer of Health's action in stopping the man from working has approval.

Sanitary Inspector.

Regarding disinfections, these were of dwelling houses as under:-

2 in September for diphtheria; 2 diphtheria and 6 scarlet fever in October; 11 diphtheria and 2 scarlet fever in November; 2 schools were closed and thoroughly disinfected on account of the outbreak of diphtheria.

18th DECEMBER 1939 (T.R.D.C.)

Correspondence.

Letter from the Ministry of Health intimating the Minister's approval to the immunisation against diphtheria of the poorer inhabitants of the district. In this connection the Medical Officer of Health pointed out the difficulties and enormous amount of extra work this would involve.

Resolved that the matter be left with the Medical Officer of Health.

CHAPTER THREE
January 1940 to December 1940

FOOD RATIONING BEGAN

JANUARY 1940

Food rationing began in January 1940 and continued into the 1950s. The food ration, which varied but slightly, for one person for one week is given below.

Two ounces of tea.

Eight ounces of sugar.

Four ounces of bacon.

Four ounces of lard or margarine.

One shilling and two pence worth of meat (13 ounces).

Cheese ration varied two to three ounces per week

Each month a person was allowed one egg, one packet of dried egg, eight ounces of jam and 12 ounces of chocolates or sweets. Also controlled was milk - averaged two to two and a half pints a week. Bread, potatoes and fresh vegetables were not officially rationed but fresh vegetables were scarce.

Packet foods and tinned foods were issued on points. A person was allowed twenty points every four weeks. Twenty-four points enabled a pound tin of stewed steak to be purchased. A tin of Grade Three salmon, half a pound of chocolate biscuits, a packet of breakfast cereal, one pound of rice, one tin of pilchards (if available) came to twenty points.

Campaigns were launched to make the best use of food available and a 'Dig For Victory' campaign encouraged people to grow their own vegetables and fruit.

15th JANUARY 1940 (T.R.D.C.)

Salvaging of Waste Paper, etc.

I have had quotations from firms who are prepared to purchase baled waste paper and cardboard in four to five ton consignments. As the material will be required to be stored until a five ton load has accumulated, I ask permission to erect a further shed. The shed already erected is for the storage of bottles and jars, etc. for which there is a market, also for the safe keeping of the non-ferrous metals, i.e. aluminium, brass etc., until a sufficient weight has been accumulated for sale. This is, however, at present completely filled with waste paper and cardboard.

Y.M.C.A. Hut, Castlegarth, Thirsk.

Mr. Ivan Smith has submitted plans showing the arrangement and site of a proposed Y.M.C.A. hut.

3ʳᵈ FEBRUARY 1940 (D/S)
Liver said to be unfit for food.

Thirsk butchers ask for explanation.

When the Buying and Finance Committee of the Thirsk Meat Traders Association met at the Three Tuns Hotel, Thirsk, on Thursday night, the secretary read a letter from the Thirsk Sanitary Inspector, (Mr. F. Metcalfe), which stated that he examined some livers in Thirsk, and these, or parts of them, were in his opinion unfit for food. He asked that it should be surrendered and the total weight surrendered to him was 35 lbs.

With regard to this weekend's supplies of meat in Thirsk, Mr. James Horner, a local butcher, stated, 'We were told on Wednesday there were only five beasts for butchers in Thirsk, but there would be plenty of frozen

meat on Friday. We rang up today (Friday), and were informed there was no frozen beef, but there would be plenty of Canterbury lamb. The local butchers then ordered 100 Canterbury lambs, but we have since been told we can only have 50.

26ᵗʰ FEBRUARY 1940 (T.R.D.C)
Evacuation.

The Clerk submitted a Circular letter from the Ministry of Health enclosing a memorandum setting out the Minister's proposals in regard to the evacuation of schoolchildren in the event of enemy air raids over certain areas. He also submitted a letter from the Ministry stating that the council was asked to provide accommodation for 1000 schoolchildren from Gateshead where necessary.

9ᵗʰ MARCH 1940 (D/S)
Topcliffe Women's Institute.

The first monthly meeting since the outbreak of war was held when Miss Rayner, Vice President, presided. As the President, Miss Pauling, has left the village, Mrs. C. Pauling, wife of the new Vicar, was appointed her successor. An egg collection for local hospitals is to be taken at the April meeting. The Hon. Treasurer, Mrs. Barningham resigned and Miss Bulmer accepted the office. Mrs. Burton won a hyacinth competition and Mrs. Taylor a musical competition. Miss Bulmer and Mrs. Taylor were the winners of a jigsaw puzzle competition arranged by Miss Dowson. Tea was served by Mrs. Clark, Mrs. Egan, Mrs. Bowen and Miss Dowson.

25ᵗʰ MARCH 1940 (T.R.D.C.)
Medical Officer of Health's Report.

The Medical Officer of Health attended and reported on the health of the District. He also reported that he had attended a Conference of Medical Officers at Northallerton to discuss the provision of 'sick bays' and 'hostels for difficult cases' under the Governments Evacuation Scheme.

Disinfections.

The three disinfections were one for diphtheria, one for scarlet fever and the third in Army Billets at the Poor Law Institution.

13ᵗʰ APRIL 1940 (D/S)
Sowerby (Thirsk).

The monthly meeting of Sowerby Women's Institute was held on Thursday in the Wesleyan Schoolroom. Mrs. Ormston presided. An address was given by Mrs. Watson of Osgoodby on the work of the Produce Guild, and she was thanked on the motion of Mrs. Cowton. Letters of thanks were read from local troops who received knitted garments from the knitting party. The hostesses were Mrs. Cowton, Mrs. Duck, Mrs. Claxton and Miss Bromby. Eggs were collected and have been given to the Lambert Memorial Hospital, Thirsk.

5ᵗʰ MAY 1940

WINSTON CHURCHILL BECAME PRIME MINISTER

6ᵗʰ MAY 1940 (T.R.D.C.)
Salvage.

During the month house to house collections have been made in Sessay, Hutton Sessay, Dalton, Topcliffe, Carlton Miniott, Sandhutton and parts of Newsham.

Mortuaries and War, Drainage.

Medical Officer:- From conversations I have had with the principal Contractors in Thirsk and Sowerby it appears that none carry any large amount of timber, etc. as they are unable to get same. Regarding the Mortuary Building, the only one I can at present submit is the old Marine Store Building in Long Street. This is a three storey building having a floor area of 35ft. by 25ft. and height of 10ft.7ins. The objection to this building would be it abuts on dwelling houses on one side. Otherwise access is fairly good and there is water supply and drainage facility.

11th MAY 1940 (D/S)
Cricket Begins at Thirsk.

This week saw the opening of the cricket season at Thirsk. Practice began at the Thirsk Athletic Club's nets in readiness for a series of fixtures which have been arranged over Whitsuntide. Arrangements have been made to adapt the sport to war conditions, and although League cricket is out of the question for the time being, an interesting programme of Wednesday and week-end friendly fixtures is being arranged. Members of the forces, too, are being encouraged to take advantage of the Club's cricket, tennis and bowling facilities, and it is hoped to arrange matches with teams from the services.

15th MAY 1940 (T.R.D.C.)
Mr. Savage's Chrysanthemums.

I have made further inspection of Mr.Savage's bed of chrysanthemums on his allotment in Topcliffe Road, and regret to state that none of these plants appear to be living.

Recommended that Mr. Savage be paid one pound.(£1).

ON THE KITCHEN FRONT

The Ministry of Food asks every housewife

TO READ

Most newspapers and magazines are running special wartime cookery features. Read them regularly. It is a good plan to cut out the items that interest you and keep them handy in a scrap book.

TO LISTEN

Broadcasts have been arranged to give all the latest practical information about buying, preparing and cooking food. Look out for them. They tell what foods are in season and how they can be used.

TO WATCH

Simple demonstrations in cookery and meal planning are being arranged up and down the country. Ask for particulars from your local Food Office or Education Authority. Go along and take your friends.

ISSUED BY THE MINISTRY OF FOOD

1939/40

Bob Smith. Resident of Thirsk.

As a sixteen year old, along with two others, we were enlisted as messengers for the Civil Defence. Whenever the siren went, usually in the middle of the night, we had to report, with our bikes, to the office which was over the Midland Bank. A Mr. Billy Ward was in charge. He lived in Station Road and on several occasions I had to go and get him as he hadn't heard the siren. This was probably my most important task as at that time nothing very exciting happened in Thirsk.

Our uniform was a black beret and an armband.

In 1942 I was called up for the army and enlisted in the Royal Signals and trained as a Special Wireless Operator intercepting enemy messages and passing them to Intelligence to break down the code.

26ᵗʰ MAY to 2ⁿᵈ JUNE 1940
EVACUATION OF DUNKIRK
338,226 MEN EVACUATED

10ᵗʰ JUNE 1940 (T.R.D.C.)
Auxiliary Fire Service.

The Financial Officer reported that he had now received the necessary maps to complete the Council's Auxiliary Fire Brigade Scheme and that he had conferred with the Chairman before asking Mr. Robson of the Water Company to fill in the details on the map.

10ᵗʰ JUNE 1940
ITALY DECLARES WAR ON FRANCE AND BRITAIN

1ˢᵗ JULY 1940 (T.R.D.C.)
Salvage.

Sales for the month of June are approximately £100.

Waste material being sold being:-

Scrap metal 25 tons 11 cwt.

Non-ferrous metals, (brass, copper, aluminium)

Mixed paper and books. 10tons 18 cwt.

Mixed rags and woollens approx. 9 cwt.

House to house collections of Waste Materials have now been completed in most of the larger villages, 32 in fact have been done. Special visits have been made to those houses in villages which only comprise a few houses, but in view of the new compulsory requirements as to the salvaging of paper, rags and bones, all villages will in future be dealt with.

Correspondence.

Letter from the Gateshead Director of Education asking if the Council could arrange for housing a small special school of physically defective children.

Recommended that he be informed that there is no accommodation available in the district.

Fire Brigade.

The Financial Officer reported that a Conference had been held at Middlesbrough to consider the setting up of Mutual Assistance Schemes as outlined in the Fire Brigade Act 1938. After a general discussion it was recommended that the Council enter into Mutual Assistance Agreements for fire protection with the Northallerton and Ripon Fire Authorities forthwith.

15ᵗʰ July 1940
Correspondence.

a) Circular letter from the County Council stating that circumstances do not permit them to carry out works of surveying and strengthening cellars, etc. for the provision of domestic shelters and that this work must be carried out by the District Council where permitted by the Regional Commissioner.

b) Letter from the Ministry of Health stating that the Thirsk Rural District Council was to receive a further 1,000 unaccompanied children from Gateshead, 500 under plan B and 500 under plan C.

c) Letter from the County Council stating that they had received a report on samples of water taken from the Water Course (No.3) in the parish of Sessay showing pollution and asking for the Council's next observations.

Evacuation.

Mr. E. Reed. Hon. Billeting Officer submitted the following report.
On Sunday 7ᵗʰ July 1940
    189 Elementary children were billeted in the country.
    106 Secondary children were billeted in Thirsk and Sowerby.
     81 Elementary children were billeted in Sowerby.
On Monday 8ᵗʰ July 1940
    210 children were billeted in the country.
     97 Elementary children were billeted in Thirsk.
A total of 683.

In addition teachers were billeted in respective parishes. I should like to thank the Billeting Officers and the Voluntary helpers and police who so ably assisted me in the billeting of the children. As a general rule the householders throughout the area received the children willingly and very few complaints have been received from either the children or the householders; of course there are still some questions to be settled not only people who have taken the children out of sympathy although they have not the necessary accommodation and these are being attended to as quickly as possible.

On the other hand several people who have accommodation either locked their doors or refused to billet children and feeling is running high and I ask the Council to take legal proceedings against these people. The best way to deal with this would be to give the tribunal executive powers to deal with these cases as they arrive.

Resolved that the tribunal be given executive powers to take legal proceedings against people refusing to take evacuees.

The necessary bedding is available on application and practically all such applications have been dealt with.

20th July 1940 (D/S)
Women's Institutes.

Thirkleby with Bagby. The monthly meeting was held at Spital Hill by invitation of the President, Mrs. C. Harris. In the absence of the speaker, Mrs. Godman, Miss Downie gave an A.R.P. talk on high explosive bombs, which proved of great interest. Games and competitions were held in the garden. A meeting was also held in Thirkleby Schoolroom at which Mrs. Elphick gave a talk on the making of pickles and chutneys. Mrs. Harris presided, and the hostesses were Miss Snowball, Miss Hylton, and Miss Duffield. Competitions were won by Mrs. Hylton, Mrs. Duffield and Mrs. Scatchard.

MINISTRY OF FOOD

YOUR NEW RATION BOOK

HOW TO REGISTER WITH THE SHOPS

The new Ration Books are now being distributed. As soon as you receive your new Book you must fill in the particulars as explained below, and then take the Book to the shops for fresh Registration. It has been found possible to allow *immediate* Registration, and the sooner you register the better. This is what to do :—

1 On the pages of coupons for Rationed Foods (Meat, Bacon, Butter and Sugar) you must fill in your name and address (BLOCK LETTERS) in the space provided in the centre of each page.

2 At the foot of these pages are spaces marked 'Counterfoil'. Here you must write your name and address, the date, and the name and address of the shop where you wish to buy the particular food during the six months' period beginning July 8th.

3 Inside the front cover of your Ration Book you must write the names and addresses of the shops.

4 As soon as you have done this, take the Book to each of the shops with whom you intend to register, so that they may cut out their counterfoils.

EVERYONE MUST REGISTER FOR THE NEW PERIOD

The Ministry of Food is responsible both for the supply and quality of rationed foods. No retailer is, therefore, in a better position than another to secure supplies of rationed foods, nor can one retailer promise to provide a better quality than another.

Topcliffe Fair Held as Usual.

Smaller attendance and old customs neglected.

Topcliffe Fair, shorn of much of its picturesque tradition through the passing of time, and more so this year on account of the war, was held as usual on Thursday.

The attendance and number of horses on offer were low compared with previous years, although not the smallest on record, but there was still a fair sprinkling of gypsies and 'potters' whose forefathers travelled to the Fair in the past. There was also the usual gathering of farmers and dealers.

12th AUGUST 1940 (T.R.D.C)
The Military Scavenging.

Application has been made by the Military for the council to carry out the removal of ashes from the several billets in Thirsk and Sowerby, such work to be paid for when over and above the ordinary collecting arrangements (namely more than once a week), and where carried out at premises not rated.

The military contractor who carried out the removal of privy soil has given indifferent service and I have been asked to submit an estimate for the Council to take over this work from 1st September.

16th AUGUST 1940 (T.R.D.C.)
Air Raid Precautions Scheme.

The Clerk reported that Form E.F.B.2 setting out the Council's proposed Emergency Fire Brigade's Measure had been submitted to the Home Office and had received the following reply.

7th August 1940.

Dear Sir,

A preliminary examination of your Council's air raid precautions scheme has now been carried out, and I enclose, in duplicate, a memorandum setting out a number of points on which further information is desired or which appear to call for further consideration. It would be convenient if you would enter the replies and observations, so far as space permits, on one of the copies, and where this is not convenient, include them in a separate report.

I am to express appreciation of the care with which it is evident that the Scheme has been prepared.

As regards the provision of the emergency appliances, the Minister will be prepared in due course, to allocate for the Council's use in connection with the scheme 1 large and 1 light trailer pump and manual and hand pumps to such numbers as may be fixed when further information indicated in the accompanying Memorandum has been received.

In the meantime, the Minister will authorise the issue, for the Council's use in connection with the emergency measures, in addition to the appliances already issued, 1 large trailer pump; this will be issued as supplies become available from the manufacturers, and will be part of the allocation mentioned above. He would also be able to accept for purposes of Exchequer grant the reasonable cost of recruiting and training Auxiliary Firemen and members of fire parties, up to the numbers of 40 and 100 respectively.

Air Raid Precautions.

The Honorary Air Raid Precautions Officer reported that it was necessary for one of the report centre controllers' private telephone to be extended to his bedside.

Recommended that this be agreed to, the Council to pay the cost of such extension.

BATTLE OF BRITAIN

The battle of Britain was an attempt by the German Air Force to gain command of the skies over Britain. Some 1,485 German aircraft crossed the Channel on 13th August, 1940 in an attempt to defeat the R.A.F. The battle continued over Southern England until middle to late September with victory going to England and her allies.

7th September 1940 (D/S)
When The Sirens Are Sounded.
The sirens do not sound before there is need for the people in a given area to be warned of the enemy raiders' approach. That is the settled policy of the Government, and it has been chosen as better than a system of extended warnings over areas to which a raider might go. Hitler does not expect to do as much damage to property as hindrance to war production and transport by his raids. It defeats Hitler's purpose to warn only those towns towards which enemy aircraft are actually moving. Accordingly at many works where war material is being made systems are being devised, by means of special observation posts, which will enable war production to be maintained until in Sir John Anderson's words, 'it is clear that an enemy attack is actually imminent in their area.'

9th September 1940 (T.R.D.C.)
Mr. G.A.Lomas raised the question of the provision of public shelter in the Market Place at Thirsk and after a general discussion on the matter it was recommended that application be made to the Regional Officer for permission to erect a public shelter in the Market Place at Thirsk.

28th September 1940 (D/S)
Shelter Problem In Rural Areas.
Thirsk's problem of finding air raid shelters, if needed, for people attending the weekly market, is one which must be common to many rural towns in the North Riding. In the light of information before Thirsk Rural District Council this week the best plan at that centre would seem to be a scheme for utilising the cellars of premises surrounding the Market Place, many of which have direct access from the street. The cellars would probably serve an equally useful purpose as a specific shelter built in the market - an alternative plan, which at the moment, is discounted owing to financial considerations.

7th October 1940 (T.R.D.C.)
Salvage and repair of War Damage.
On Friday afternoon 4th instant, I attended a meeting at Easingwold in connection with the above - the matters discussed being,
  a)   salvage of property and
  b)   removal of debris and the clearance of sites.

It appears that the Council's primary duty after bombing would be

1) To save life.
2) Remove bodies.
3) Make buildings temporarily safe to prevent damage to life or limb.
4) Removal and storage of furniture and accommodation for the affected persons where necessary.

Although the Council is expected to use its own resources in this work, it is understood that where such was found impracticable and a Contractor employed, the expenditure would be recoverable.

Mortuaries.

The conversion of the slaughter house buildings in Chapel Street, Thirsk is now almost complete.

15ᵗʰ OCTOBER 1940 (E.A.M.)

Whitley Bomber, Mark 5, crashed near Grundyke Farm between Thirsk and Bagby. Two crew killed, three survived.

21ˢᵗ OCTOBER 1940 (T.R.D.C.)

The Council in Committee considered the various points arising from the enemy's recent air attack on the town. The various responsible Officers reported on the working of the Services, and answered several questions put to them by members.

The question of blackout in the town, particularly in relation to places occupied by the Military, was also considered and it was recommended :

a) That a vote of confidence in each officer concerned in the Council's Air Raid Precautions Services be moved.

b) That the Clerk write to the Ministry of Home Security, the Commanding Officer (Northern Command), and the Chief Constable, asking that immediate steps be taken to ensure compliance with the blackout regulations.

26th October 1940 (D/S)
Thirsk and 'Lights' Cases.

'Lights' cases continue to occupy the attention of magistrates in most centres, and it is becoming plainly evident that more vigorous repressive action will have to be taken if the danger arising from the carelessness of householders in this repect are to be reduced to a minimum. Longer hours of darkness obviously extend the period of risk infringement of the lighting regulations, and unless public attention is fixed more rigidly on the imperative need of a really effective blackout it is possible that this particular offence will tend to increase. Thirsk magistrates, therefore, are to be commended on the warning they gave this week to the effect that they will take a most serious view of future cases.

Bill Rukin. *Resident of Thirsk.*

On the 1st of January 1932 the Rukin family moved from Tees-side to 22, South Terrace Thirsk. New Year's Day was perhaps an odd day for moving but Bill's father was a Police Sergeant and the date was set by his superiors. Some two years later Bill enrolled as a pupil at Finkle Street School. Here he learned to read and write.

This was not the only school Bill attended. Sunday School at the Chapel on St. James Green also influenced his education. The Sunday School children were allowed to leave after the collection and this happened on Sunday, 3rd September, 1939. The news that war with Germany had been declared had quickly spread round the town and Bill was told the news on Millgate Bridge.

Thirsk, Bill recalls, quickly filled up with soldiers. These were members of the Royal Signals and other regiments and were billeted right across the town as well as on the race-course. Preparation for war was continuing alongside Bill's Dad's preparations for retirement. This meant a move to Long Street, Thirsk, and Bill's father becoming a member of the Observer Corps Volunteers, better known as 'plane spotters'. Preparations were also going ahead for Bill's entry to the Secondary School on Topcliffe Road.

Bill became a member of the Kestrel Patrol of Thirsk Scouts. This organisation taught Bill the basic rules of scouting when he promised 'to do his best, to do his duty, for God and King and to help other people at all times'. With his fellow Scouts a camp would be made in Thirkleby Woods where three old tram cars were parked in a 'U' formation. This was a semi-permanent site but latrines still had to be dug and water fetched. Dead wood was collected as all cooking was done over an open fire. Camping at Kirkdale provided another scouting adventure.

Along with other families in Thirsk, Bill's family took in an evacuee by the name of Alex Headley, who was to stay with the family for some two years.

At school the woodwork class was replaced by double gardening. Plots were dug and cultivated at the side of the school under the eagle eye of the master. At home Bill would help with the feeding of the pig (shared with the Wallace family), checking the hens, mucking out the byre where a heifer calf was housed, chopping sticks for the fire and helping to cultivate the garden. He can recall few problems with rationing.

A number of Bill's relations lived in the Dales. Here during harvest he would be sent to help on the farm. A bus ride to Northallerton, then to Richmond and finally to Muker, would be undertaken. He also helped an aunt at Gunnerside with hay-making. Here there were few mechanical aids and the work was done with horses, a reaper and a wooden rake. The hay would either be forked into barns or piked - a satisfying job.

One incident stands out in Bill's memory. On the evening of 16th October 1940, dusk was falling and Bill was at home by himself. There was a 'thump, thump, thump.' Windows shattered, the front door crashed open. Bill had experienced what it was like to be bombed. A lone German bomber had dropped a stick of bombs as it flew over the town. One fell near the railway line at Thirsk Station; another on the race-course where some soldiers were injured and some killed; one bomb demolished Squire Bell's wall; a further bomb landed on the Marage while yet another dropped on a lamp post on St. James Green. Here Mrs.Crisp was killed by shrapnel. The remaining bombs caused damage to the houses and the school in Long Street and one fell in the Rukin's field and did not explode. A frightening experience which did not deter young Bill going out looking for shrapnel - a collector's item among the boys of the town.

Laurie Jackson.

As an apprentice lift engineer working out of a branch workshop in my hometown, Leeds, we, that is myself and the lift engineer, visited and stayed overnight when required in all the principal cities and towns in Yorkshire. Our lifts were installed in a wide variety of premises from hotels to hospitals, pubs to power stations, engineering and steel works to shops and offices. We were quite surprised when the manager told us that next week we had to go to Thirsk to modernise an old platform lift in an engineering company manufacturing farm machinery. We were told that in Thirsk they didn't know there was a war on, and as we had been 'blitzed out' of our digs in Sheffield and Hull several times we were looking forward to a quiet week in a small country town.

The company where we were to work employed their own joiner, an old boy by the name of Tom, who was to supply us with any wood work we requested. Tom and his wife lived in a terraced cottage in Sowerby Lane and, as we had no accommodation arranged, offered us a double bed in their spare room for which we were very grateful.

After our evening meal, Tom and his little dog would take us for a walk in the local fields and bye-ways. Rural Thirsk on a summer's evening made a very pleasant contrast to our normal lifestyle, and on Wednesday evening Tom told us he would take us to the World's End. This intriguing statement resolved to be an old, little pub at the end of Sowerby village where we had a few beers and a pleasant evening.

Nocturnal calls of nature were catered for by means of a chamber pot under the bed and before we turned in for the night we would use this facility.

During the night the air raid sirens wailed and to the monotonous drone of German bombers we leapt out of bed in alarm.

Unfortunately the last person to use the chamber pot had failed to put it fully under the bed and the handle was protruding slightly. In his haste my bedfellow caught his foot on the handle causing the vessel and its contents to hurtle across the floor. The bomber crew were not the only 'Jerries' that were airborne that night.

Imagine our profound embarrassment and our apologies to Tom's understanding and good-natured wife and imagine the ribald comments we received from some of the workers who blamed us for the air raid and told us, in no uncertain terms, to get back to Leeds!

Hilda Chapman.

Finkle Street was one of the major roads into the town. Hilda, her sister and father and mother lived at number eighteen. On at least one occasion a 'Waltzing Matilda' tank ran into number sixteen causing a large amount of damage. After the first incident whenever tanks came down the street Hilda and others would rush into the backyard fearful of yet another crash.

The Canadian Air Force Post Office was across the street from Hilda's home. As Christmas approached Finkle Street would be blocked with trucks loading and unloading mail for the Canadians. To relieve the monotony of the work an occasional game of baseball would be organised in the street.

Various war-time fund-raising events involved the young Hilda. The 'Red Cross Pennies' raised £32.2s.1d while a concert arranged by eight Thirsk schoolchildren for the Red Cross Prisoner of War Parcels Fund realised 12/6. This would provide for the local men, Corporal Milner and Private Peacock, who were P.O.W.'s.

On the 16th October 1940, Hilda's Aunt Minnie was working in the N.A.A.F.I. on Thirsk Racecourse when a German bomber dropped bombs on the army camp. (It is said that the pilot saw flames coming from the cook-house chimney). Some of the soldiers had just come back from exercises and were about to enjoy a meal when the raid started. They grabbed the girls and tried to protect them. One soldier, Arthur Brown, fell on top of Minnie. They started to talk and then go out together. They were later married in the Salem Chapel, Finkle Street, Thirsk.

Wedding of Arthur Brown and Minnie Stuart at Salem Chapel, Note ARP Notice,
4th November, 1940

4th NOVEMBER 1940 (T.R.D.C.)
Disinfections.

The two disinfections were at dwelling houses on account of diphtheria.

War Damage.

I have to report that 144 houses have been visited in consequence of the bombing on the evening of the 16th October, only slight damage was caused at many of the houses, namely broken glass, damaged woodwork and displaced roof slates or tiles, but in some cases the damage was more serious requiring roofs to be stripped and replaced, fallen or loose ceilings to be renewed besides the repair or renewal of doors and window frames etc.

Temporary first aid repairs were carried out the day following the bombing by employment of local tradesmen who then continued with more permanent repairs. Apart from the replacement of glass, much of this permanent repair work is well in hand..

For your information I submit the following: -

Number of houses more seriously damaged but useable	36
Number of houses slightly damaged	106
Number of houses evacuated	2

Carlton Miniott.

Regarding the damage caused by enemy action to no. 4 Manfield Terrace, Carlton Miniott, on Friday night 1st instant, instructions were given the following morning to the local builder and contractor to repair roof, damaged ceiling and bedroom floor.

Air Raid Shelters.

a) That the Clerk be instructed to make application to the Ministry of Home Security for permission to provide domestic shelters in the parishes of Thirsk, Sowerby, Carlton Miniott, Topcliffe, Dalton, Skipton Bridge and Howe under the provision of Paragraph (1) Home Security Circular 163/1940.

b) That the Council employ a technical adviser to supervise the work.

11th NOVEMBER 1940 (T.R.D.C.)
Dalton and Topcliffe Water.

The Financial Officer reported that owing to the heavy usage of water by the Military Authorities the Council were now taking more than the 10 million gallons per annum, the maximum amount agreed upon by the Thirsk District Water Company. He had been in touch with Mr. Pinkney who had agreed that any excess water taken should be charged at 1s 3d per thousand gallons.

Recommended.

a) That the charge of 1s.3d per thousand gallons in excess of 10,000,000 per annum be agreed to.

b) That the Military and Air Ministry be charged 2/= per 1,000 gallons for the water with the exception of the Topcliffe Mobilisation Stores, and the charge for this was fixed at 1s.6d. per 1,000 gallons.

War Damage.

Messrs. Jackson and Sons, Builders, Thirsk, have submitted their account for repairs carried out at damaged dwelling houses on St. James Green, Thirsk, and ask for £10 on account. I beg to confirm that both first aid and repairs of a more permanent nature have been carried out by them on my instructions.

Recommended that this be agreed to.

23rd NOVEMBER 1940 (D/S)
Darlington Motorist fined at Thirsk.

An appreciation that the police had a 'full time job at the moment', and an apology for any trouble he had caused them, was expressed by a Darlington commercial traveller in a letter to the Thirsk Bench, read on Monday. The motorist was fined £1 for failing to immobilise his car at Carlton Miniott.

30th November 1940 (D/S)
Winter Hospitality For the Troops.

The appeal made by the Secretary for War for the co-ordination and extension of welfare schemes designed to provide hospitality for men in the Services during the winter months will inevitably bring an overwhelming response. It is essential however, that local authorities, to whom the appeal has been directed, should take immediate steps to initiate a plan of campaign based on the simple, yet very practical plan that Mr. Eden has outlined. The organisation of winter hospitality for the troops is as essential in villages as in towns.'

16th December 1940 (T.R.D.C.)

Letter from the Northern Command Headquarters intimating that there is no evidence that the lights or fires from the cookhouse on the race-course contributed to the air raid on 16th October last, and, suggesting that the police will assist by bringing any infringement of Blackout regulations to the Military Commander responsible.

Letter from the Ministry of Home Security referring to Circular no. 218/1940, and stating that he is ready to arrange for the delivery of stirrup hand pumps, to be sold under the terms of the above circular at £1 each.

MINISTRY **MF** OF FOOD

THE WEEK'S

FOOD FACTS № 10

Turn on your wireless at 8.15 every morning to hear useful hints and recipes

HERE is *health* advice, *efficiency* advice and even *beauty* advice—all in one message from the Scientific Adviser to the Ministry of Food.

"To keep fighting fit during the winter we must have a healthy diet. And that diet must include plenty of 'protective' foods. These protective foods—which are listed below—are so called because they guard us from many illnesses. They help us to maintain our efficiency and keep mentally alert. Eat more of these foods. Your resistance to strain and fatigue will be stronger—and incidentally, your complexion will be clearer."

ON THE KITCHEN FRONT

CHIEF PROTECTIVE FOODS

Milk	Potatoes
Butter or Margarine	Green Vegetables (fresh or canned but not dried)
Cheese	Salads
Eggs	Fruit (fresh or canned but not dried)
Herrings (fresh, canned or salt)	
Salmon (fresh or canned)	Carrots
	Tomatoes
Liver	Wholemeal Bread

SOUP FOR AIR-RAIDS
Try to make soup every day so that you always have some to heat up in an emergency. A hot drink works wonders for the nerves at a time of shock or strain—for this reason.

After a shock, the blood pressure and the temperature of the body tend to fall. A hot drink, even if only hot water, helps to restore them and prevent that sick, faint feeling. Nothing could be better than hot vegetable soup as this is nourishing as well as soothing. Prepare and cut up 2 or 3 carrots, 2 onions, ½ small swede and if possible 2 or 3 sticks of celery. Make 1 oz. dripping very hot in your saucepan. Put in the vegetables and cook for a few minutes. Season with salt and pepper. Add 2 pints hot water and bring to the boil. Put in 2 ozs. rice or pearl barley, cover, and simmer for 2 hours. More water may be added if necessary. A little chopped parsley just before serving is a pleasant addition.

APPLE MARMALADE
Everyone with a plentiful supply of apples should make this marmalade. It's good to eat and simple to prepare. Peel, core and quarter 6 lbs. cooking apples. Simmer till soft with just enough water to prevent them from burning. Add 3 lbs. sugar and ¼ teaspoonful powdered cinnamon. Boil steadily till the marmalade thickens (about 20 minutes). This marmalade lasts only a month or two.

THE MINISTRY OF FOOD, LONDON, S.W.1

28ᵗʰ December 1940 (D/S)

Thirsk Area's Great Effort for the Red Cross.

Generous donors and bidders. £1,500 realised.

A determined and successful bid to beat all neighbouring efforts of the kind on behalf of the Red Cross Agricultural Fund was made by the Thirsk Branch of the National Farmers' Union and the Young Farmers' Club on Monday by a sale of livestock and farm and dairy produce, to which owners and others from a wide area gave ready and very generous support.

THIRSK.

GREAT AUCTION SALE ON BEHALF OF THE RED CROSS AGRICULTURE FUND.

(ORGANISED by THIRSK N.F.U. and THIRSK Y.F.C.).

MONDAY NEXT, DECEMBER 23rd, 1940.

To Be Opened By

MAJOR R. H. TURTON, M.P.

At 10.30 a.m., at

THE SALE ROOMS, THIRSK.

A GOLD HALF-SOVEREIGN; a Large Quantity of Dressed and Live Geese, Ducks, Chickens and other Fowls; about 3 Tons of Potatoes and Carrots, in lots to suit purchasers; 215 Day-old Chicks; Rabbits, Apples, Honey, etc.

AT THIRSK FARMERS' AUCTION MART, STATION ROAD.

At 1.30 p.m.

3 FAT CATTLE; 1 In-calf Cow; 7 Store Cattle, including a Highland Bullock; 10 Veal and Holding Calves; 70 Sheep, including Pedigree Wens, Shearling Gimmer, Down Gimmers and a Suffolk Ram; 80 Pigs,

---

CHAPTER FOUR
January to December 1941

12ᵗʰ JANUARY 1941 (T.R.D.C.)
Sanitary Inspectors Report.

Food condemned 80 lbs of sausages (unsound).

Disinfections;- Scarlet fever - 2, Infantile Paralysis - 1, Scabies - 1, Tuberculosis - 1.

Matters for the Committee.

Joint application made by Messrs. Rogers and S. Lofthouse, Sowerby, Team Labour Contractors to the Council to be paid £1 per day for supply of Horse and Men from 1ˢᵗ. January 1941. The application is stated to be based on the high cost of living expenses in connection with the feeding of horses and maintenance.

13ᵗʰ JANUARY 1941 (Diary).

To-day at about twelve o'clock an R.A.F. bomber crashed near Topcliffe. Five of the crew were killed.

21ˢᵗ JANUARY 1941 (T.R.D.C.)

Application has been made by a Corporal in the Military Police for the Public Conveniences to be kept open after black-out hours, in order to prevent nuisance being caused in the streets. I have explained the reason for the premises having to be closed, but the Police state that they cannot take action against soldiers causing a nuisance where there is no facility available.

Recommended that further information on the matter be obtained.

27ᵗʰ JANUARY 1941 (T.R.D.C.)
Correspondence.

Letter from the Minister of Home Security pointing out the necessity for the immediate organisation of parties to locate and extinguish incendiary bombs, and it was resolved that application be made for an order, investing the Council with compulsory powers in this connection for the parishes of Thirsk and Sowerby.

Further resolved that each householder in Thirsk and Sowerby be provided with a bag of sand for

extinguishing incendiary bombs and that sand be provided also for the rest of the Rural Areas.

Circular from the Ministry of Health delegating the powers under the Defence Regulations to Local Authorities, whereby Billeting Officers can now enter and inspect premises in which it is proposed to billet evacuated persons.

9th FEBRUARY 1941 (Diary).

Last night enemy aircraft dropped bombs on a Yorkshire Town. No damage done. Our lights in Topcliffe went out and we heard one bomb drop.

10th FEBRUARY 1941 (T.R.D.C.)

Letter from the Air Ministry asking if it was possible for this Council to supply 20,000 gallons of water per day from the Dalton and Topcliffe Water Supply. Recommended that they be informed that the capacity of the Dalton and Topcliffe main was not sufficient to allow any further consumers.

Fire Watching.

After a general discussion on the position of this Council with regard to fire watching it was recommended that a sub-committee consisting of Thirsk and Sowerby Members together with the Hon. A.R.P. Officer, Mr. A.S.C. Broadway, to consider the question in so far as it relates to the parishes of Thirsk and Sowerby.

That the Clerk send a letter to the Chairman of each Parish Council and Parish Meeting asking if they would be prepared to formulate a scheme and put same in operation in each of their respective parishes as the Council were of the opinion that better results would be obtained in this manner than by the Council administering it themselves.

22nd FEBRUARY 1941 (D/S)

War Savings Drive in Thirsk Area.

Need of More Groups.

War Weapons Week Date.

A well-attended meeting was held at the Church House, Thirsk, on Friday, 14th inst., to inaugurate an intensive war savings effort in the Thirsk and Sowerby area.

The president, (Mr. G.A. Lomas, J.P.), who was supported by L.H.Jenkins (Assistant Commissioner), and Mr. Houston (Deputy Commissioner), explained that there were at present existing 54 savings groups as against 23 in 1939. It was necessary that existing groups should be given every encouragement to increase their membership and there was an urgent need for many more groups to be formed in places of employment, shops, farms and any similar community.

> THIRSK AND SOWERBY WAR WEAPONS WEEK.
>
> MAY 24th to 31st.
>
> A MEETING Specially Arranged for the Convenience of Business and Professional Men, will be held in the Toc H Rooms, Market Place, Thirsk, on FRIDAY, March 14th. at 3.0 p.m. And another Meeting, designed for the Convenience of the General Public, will be held at the Salem Schoolroom Finkle Street, Thirsk, on the Same Evening, at 7 30 o'clock.
>
> GEORGE A LOMAS. President.
> Rev. GEORGE A. STEEL. Sec.

There was a large number of people already purchasing war savings certificates or bonds through their respective banks or the Post Office who were not necessarily attached to any group. Apart from these there were still many people who were not at present in the scheme at all and it was these people they wished to reach and enrol.

It had therefore been decided to organise a band of collectors who would each be responsible for a street or portion of a street, a cluster of cottages or farms, or any small community of people. The method most suited to this purpose was the savings stamp scheme. These were of 6d and 2s 6d denomination and the purchasing of these stamps was both a receipt and a record of the transaction. Money collected in this way would be used to purchase national savings certificates or defence bonds for the lenders and it was important for these people to know that they could, if so desired, obtain repayment of the money subscribed at any period. It was therefore necessary that the committee should obtain the names of responsible persons who were willing to act as local secretaries or collectors.

Success of Savings Groups.

Where savings groups have been formed they have been very successful. A collector dealing with a series of small hamlets stated that originally two pounds worth of stamps were sold weekly, but now the sale of stamps had risen to £20 per week.

With proper co-operation the Thirsk Committee feel that the effort now to be made will achieve success. It is hoped that the names of a sufficient number of collectors will be registered so that the whole area can be dealt with and everybody given an opportunity to do his or her part to help.

A War Weapons Week is to be organised to take place from 24th May to 31st. During that week the Army will be asked to demonstrate a captured German 'plane and other events of interest will be organised. The sum to be aimed for will be £30,000.

An executive committee as well as a general committee will be formed and the Rev. G.A. Steel has promised to act as campaign secretary.

J. Terry Barker. *Resident of Thirsk*

I was born on the 6th of January 1933 in the small hamlet of Kirby Knowle at the foot of the Hambleton Hills. Kirby Knowle was part of the Kirby Knowle Estate and consisted of twelve houses together with seven surrounding farms. There was neither pub nor shop in the village but a school and a sub Post Office could be found about a mile away on the road towards Upsall. All the villagers, with the exception of my father, were employed by the Estate. In the big house lived the Major. This was the only house which had electricity which was provided by a 5 h.p. Lister engine. All the other houses in the village used paraffin lamps and candles. No sewage system was installed in the village. The privies (toilets), were at the bottom of the garden, some double seaters, some single. These were earth closets with an ash pit at the side. Ashes from the fires were deposited here. The privies were emptied by a local farmer using a horse and cart and contents were spread on the land.

Firewood used to be collected from the nearby wood when felling was taking place, (hand saw and axe).

Mother used to bake bread in the old black leaded oven at the side of the fire. At the other side of the fire was a water boiler with a hinged lid. This boiler had to be kept full of water at all times when the fire was lit or the cast iron tank would have cracked with disastrous results. Hot water from the side boiler was used for washing and was ladled from the boiler with a ladle tin. Any water removed was promptly replaced from the bucket in the scullery. Friday night was bath night and the fire for the copper boiler in the wash house had to be lit in the late afternoon while the copper boiler was filled with several buckets of water.

Eight o' clock was bath time and the large galvanised bath was brought in and placed in front of the fire then filled with water from the copper. A bath was then taken and then off to bed.

My father had one of the first wirelesses in the village. It consisted of a large box with valves inside and two dials and three switches on the front. The three switches were an 'on' and 'off' switch, a long or medium wave switch, while the third switch was for lights to make tuning easier. This latter was never used for the accumulator would run down too quickly. The aerial for the wireless was fixed to a tree opposite the house and had to be adjusted according to the weather. The accumulators were recharged at Smirthwaites in the High Street, Northallerton.

Only two programmes could be received on the wireless, these being the Home Service and the Light Programme. I remember listening to the news, Workers' Playtime, Dick Barton, Special Agent, I.T.M.A. with Tommy Handley, Family Favourites and Into Battle. I can also remember Lord Haw Haw breaking into programmes with his well-known words, 'Germany calling, Germany calling,' then giving out propaganda against the British.

The first job I can remember being carried out on the Estate was the planting of the hillside behind the village. A tree nursery in the village provided the trees which were loaded on to a horse which had been fitted with two saddle bags. The loads of young trees were then delivered up the hill to the planters.

School life for me began in January 1938 when I became a pupil at the local school. The schoolroom was heated by a coke stove surrounded by a fire-guard. It was the cleaner's job to trim the paraffin lamps and to get the stove going. The classroom had high windows, dual desks and a blackboard and easel. The village school had one teacher and some twenty pupils varying in age from five to fourteen. The cleaner used to travel to school on her bicycle from the next village. I remember that the cycle was fitted with calcium carbide lamps. To extinguish these lamps the water supply had to be cut off. One day she removed one from her cycle and turned off the water supply thereby extinguishing the light. As she went to turn off the other it burst into flames and burnt out in the school playground. An exciting incident in a young boy's day!

The school teacher lived in the school house at the bottom of the village. The school was split into three classes, infants, juniors, and seniors, with two rows of desks for each. The school consisted of two rooms separated by a removable wooden partition. Only the big room was used for teaching. The other small room was used only when the 'Nit nurse' visited or the school doctor or dentist. No water was piped into school. Water for drinks was brought indoors in a bucket from a tap situated near the school yard railings. The senior girls used to do this chore.

Every school day the first chore was to fill the kettle and set it on the stove to boil for playtime. Everyone at school had a small beaker with a measure mark on the inside. At playtime everyone received a beaker of Horlicks and never a fraction above the mark on the beaker.

Sanitation at school was the same as the cottages, earth closets and ash pits. These were cleared out by a local farmer. School life was routine but certain jobs had to be done to meet wartime regulations. I remember everyone in school having to help with sticking brown tape on all the windows in a criss-cross pattern fairly closely spaced, the reason being that if a bomb dropped and an explosion took place the glass would shatter but be held in place by the tape. Gas masks were issued and these had to be carried to school every day. Regular tests were also carried out on the wearing of the gas mask. We soon got used to this new way of living.

Life at school was fairly routine until the arrival of the evacuees from Newcastle and Gateshead. The village school was brought into full use at this time (1939/1940). The unused room through the partition was made into infants, the big room was split in two by a portable screen, one part being juniors, and the other seniors. Two new teachers arrived with the evacuees, a master to teach seniors, our teacher to teach juniors and the new lady teacher the infants. The steady mundane life of the country was brought to an abrupt end. Evacuee pupils arrived late, played truant, argued with teachers and in one case violence against a teacher was used. This kind of behaviour had not been seen in the local community. The master kept law and order by use of the strap and, believe me, it worked. Those at the receiving end did not go back for more. The trouble makers did not like country life and soon filtered back to Tyneside leaving the rest to a more settled life.

My brother and I were told on the 3rd of September,1939, that war had broken out. The first thought of my younger brother and I was that we must not go up into the woods in case we met a German.

At this time the main houses on the country estates were taken over by the army. Cowesby Hall, New Buildings, Kirby Knowle and part of Upsall Castle were all put to military use. The big house at the top of the village was used to accommodate the Officer-in-Charge of the army in the area. He had a batman who used to drive a utility truck. This vehicle was used to travel to the camp at New Buildings to collect supplies. We boys used to ride with the batman to the camp and when passing the guardroom at the entrance to the camp we had to duck down under the dashboard so as not to be seen. We used to have a good chat with all the soldiers.

Two of the local farmers used to go on up to the camp with horse and trap to collect swill and waste from the kitchens on a daily basis. One Saturday night liquid refreshment was required by the farmers so bicycles out and off to the nearest pub. This meant going past the guardroom and on to the public road. After several pints and arriving back at the guardroom satisfactory reasons for going on to the camp were not given, so the two happy farmers were arrested and put in the guardroom for the night. Next morning big problems arose because the swill had not been collected. After hurried investigations the farmers were traced to the guardroom and promptly released with an apology but told to get on with their vital job.

The army gave us youngsters in the village many hours of interest. Tanks, guns, lorries, Bren gun carriers, field guns and marching troops were everyday occurrences. Soldiers in groups of eight used to run along the road with two men holding the handle at the rear of a field gun and three at each side with ropes attached to the hubs of the wheels pulling the gun at running speed with officers running alongside shouting instructions. I remember that one day a tank ran off the road just out of the village and was completely bogged down. Word about this soon got round so at lunch time while the teacher was at home for her lunch most of us schoolchildren decided to go and watch the tank being recovered. The event took longer than anticipated and most of the watching schoolchildren arrived back at school at 3.15. School finished at 3.30 and this left just enough time to get into big trouble for leaving the school yard.

One morning mother called me earlier than usual and said, 'Come and look at the moor.' Behind the village the land rises sharply to form part of the Hambleton Hills. Along the skyline the whole moor was ablaze. Part way down was a young plantation which had to be protected. All the estate men were sent to dig a trench to stop the fire spreading. While this task was being undertaken a detachment of American troops was sent to fight the fire. They helped with the trench and stopped the fire spreading to the plantation.

In the field behind the village the Americans set up a camp. They dug trenches in the ground and put some metal grids on top of the trenches with heaters underneath to do the cooking. We youngsters thought the Americans were great. They gave us chocolate. The following morning the fire broke out again and once again the Americans and estate workers thought it was out. This happened a third time until the fire was finally extinguished. The Americans stayed the next day and moved out the following day much to the dismay of the local girls. The fire was supposed to have been started by a German incendiary bomb.

Another incident of my boyhood was getting up one morning and looking out of the bedroom window towards Cowesby. There, fast in the wood, was a huge barrage balloon. This meant a quick breakfast then with my brother and on our bikes we went to investigate. We arrived at the wood, left our bikes by the road and walked up to the balloon. It was huge and held fast in the trees by its trailing and twisted cables. We left the wood and returned home. The army mounted a guard round the balloon and cordoned off the area until the balloon was deflated and taken away. It was believed that the barrage balloon had broken its moorings and had then drifted south until the cables snagged on the trees.

One Saturday morning I was doing my chores. One of my jobs was to walk to the bottom of the village to collect milk and eggs from the local smallholder. When halfway down the village I could hear an aeroplane coming from the direction of Cowesby. It seemed very low when suddenly there was a loud 'thud' then silence. I presumed the plane had crashed. I took the milk home and told mother what I had heard, (took a lecture from mother about being careful), collected my bike and my brother and I went to investigate. We rode to Cowesby but could see nothing so we left our bikes by the side of the road and climbed to the top of the moor. Looking back towards Cowesby Hall in a small valley was the crashed plane, vapour and smoke were hissing out in several places. We climbed down to the moor to have a closer look but did not get too close in case of fire. The ground in the area was covered with machine gun ammunition. The plane had come down in a boggy valley and had gouged a track where the four engines and the fuselage had dug in as it crashed. The stricken plane was a Halifax bomber. We made our way back to the road and our bikes and were riding back home when we were overtaken by the fire engine. It pulled up and the men on board asked if we knew where a plane had crashed. We told them exactly where it was but said there was no way the fire engine could get to the crash. They went to investigate; we went home to report to mother what we had seen. I remember the fire engine was painted grey and had N.F.S. (National Fire Service) painted on the doors of the cab.

I remember the formation of the Home Guard and going with the locals on some of their exploits which included target practice. In the very early days before rifles and Bren guns were issued they used to practise drill using broom shanks. Sunday mornings were practice days and mock battles were arranged with other groups. At other times rifle shooting practice used to take place on a range made at the foot of the Hambleton Hills near the road between Kirby Knowle and Boltby. Early on Sunday mornings I used to go with the gamekeeper along the footpath which runs from Kirby Knowle part way up the Hambleton Hills and then to Boltby putting up red flags warning anyone walking between the villages that shooting practice was taking place.

When air raids were imminent the siren in Thirsk used to sound. This meant taking extra precautions like checking the blackout in case any lights were showing and preparing to take cover. This was under the stairs as no air raid shelters were available. At times when the siren sounded I used to go outside the house with father and watch the planes overhead. Searchlights were criss-crossing the sky trying to get a plane in their beam. When they did another searchlight used to lock on to them as well and hopefully an Anti Aircraft gun could bring the plane down. One night when watching, the searchlight at Felixkirk locked on to a German plane and the plane dived down the beam using its guns to put the searchlight out. It then dropped several bombs in that area.

On summer evenings cricket used to be played in the village. We used to watch the bombers taking off and circling until all the planes were airborne and in formation. The sky used to be virtually black with the sheer number of planes on their way to bomb Germany.

Rabbits and rats were particular pests and ways were sought to control them. Rabbits ran rampant all over the area. As the fields were ploughed out and cereals were sown some forty per cent of the crop was eaten by rabbits. Something had to be done.

Do you remember when the headlines said—

"No potatoes for this Sunday's joint"

While thousands of housewives enjoyed another little grumble, the wiser families who had dug for victory enjoyed their Sunday joint with all the potatoes and other vegetables they wanted. Learn from experience. To be sure of the family's vegetables, you must grow them yourselves—women and older children as well as men. If you haven't a garden, ask your Local Council for an allotment. Start to

DIG FOR VICTORY NOW!

POST THIS COUPON NOW *(Unsealed envelope, 1d. stamp)*

TO MINISTRY OF AGRICULTURE, HOTEL LINDUM, ST. ANNES-ON-SEA, LANCS.
Please send me copies of free pictorial leaflets, "How to Dig" and "How to Crop"

NAME ....

ADDRESS ....
B.99

ISSUED BY THE MINISTRY OF AGRICULTURE

IT'S DOING **HITLER'S** WORK

KILL THAT RAT!

Here in Britain is an enemy army of Rats living on us, devouring huge quantities of food, every ounce of which is precious in war time. Kill these pests now and stop this waste.

When rabbit warrens were found they were targeted for ferreting. This usually took place on Saturday afternoons. One Saturday afternoon the farmer, the gamekeeper, my brother and myself went to a warren behind the village near a big oak tree. All the holes were netted - we knew that many rabbits had gone to ground. A ferret was put down the holes and the rabbits started trying to escape but ran into the nets. These were caught and killed by the farmer and the keeper. When no more ran out the men listened and they could hear where the rabbits were. Digging started and by the end of the day a harvest had been gathered to be sold at Monday's market in Thirsk.

Ratting was another pursuit we followed. Paradise Farm was the venue when the farmer would invite us lads down to help kill the rats. The grain barn was the best area and our weapons were stout sticks. The farmer had devised a method of 'ticing the rats from their holes then blocking the holes up to prevent a retreat. The slaughter would then begin. Our largest haul on such a night was eighty three rats. In spite of this bumper number killed there were always others to take their place.

My father worked as manager for the North Riding of Yorkshire War Agricultural Executive Committee, (W.A.R.A.G.). His office was in Boroughbridge Road, Northallerton and was once machine gunned by a German Messerschmitt. Fortunately no-one was injured. The depot of W.A.R.A.G. was full of tractors, implements, lorries, vans, bulldozers and cars. I used to go out on deliveries all over the North Riding with one of the lorry drivers delivering appliances and tractors to farms.

In 1944 I passed the 11 plus examination. This allowed me to go to the Grammar School and because father worked in Northallerton I was allowed to go to Northallerton Grammar School instead of Thirsk. I was at the Grammar School until I passed my Matriculation Certificate.

I used to come down to Thirsk market and watch the horses and traps fill up one side of the Market Place. The horses would be tethered in various pubs while people went about their business. Horses and traps were slowly replaced by mechanised vehicles. Entrance to the Market Place was made difficult by the building of concrete tank barriers. This was in case the Germans invaded. Also by the side of such barriers were forty -five gallon drums filled with concrete. These were to be pushed into the roads to hinder any invaders. Such obstacles could be found near the bridge in Finkle Street, opposite Thirsk Hall, at Town End and the Marage.

Kirby Knowle had been transformed by the erection of Nissen huts. The first huts were used by the army. Many fields were full of tanks. The fields had been covered with stone from Boltby Quarry before the tanks were parked. The Village Hall was used as a Y.M.C.A. and a N.A.A.F.I. Most of the ladies of the village worked at different times in the Y.M.C.A. and their work was much appreciated by the soldiers. Other functions were held in the Village Hall - concerts, dances and social activities. On one occasion Evelyn Laye (a singer of some repute) performed there. The music for such events was often performed by local dance bands. Such bands included the Night Hawks under the leadership of Dick Bainbridge; the Hazel Nuts under Jazzy Knowlson, while Gladys Robinson's band was known as the Nightjars.

Another influence on my young life were the prisoners of war. At first the majority were Germans and they used to be taken round the farms by lorry, from their camp at Boltby, to work. As regulations relaxed they were allowed to cycle without supervision. Italian P.O.Ws were another group. Among the group were two 'wrong 'uns' who were taken away by the Military Police. A number of prisoners of war stayed in the area after the war and I remember how some of the prisoners would unravel hessian sacks then weave and knit them into slippers. A number of P.O.W.s were skilled at making toys.

Food rationing did not prove such a problem to those of us who lived in the country. Milk, eggs, butter and bacon were generally freely available. Some of our relatives farmed in the area and when we visited we always returned with a side of bacon. In case we were stopped by the police our parents told us to sit on the bacon. Petrol coupons were another aspect of illegal black marketing but often the petrol was red and had we been caught the outlook was not good.

V.E.Day,(Victory in Europe), was celebrated with two days of Public Holidays. We had a huge bonfire and a big party at Knowle Hill. The Home Guard brought thunder flashes and in Kirby Knowle Victory in Europe ended with a bang.

Ann Coates. *Resident of Thirsk.*
Early War Years.

We Thirsk schoolchildren got off the bus in the village square. We headed off home in various directions. Bill Maynard retrieved his bike and set off to cycle the two miles to Oldstead where he lived on a farm. On the way something on the roadside caught his attention. He got off his bike and picked up the object. It blew some of his fingers off and he was left with a deformed hand. The object had been dropped by a German plane. We were warned again - never pick up anything suspicious.

A few years ago Bill was coming to Wass to visit his now retired parents. He pulled into a lay-by and died there.

About three quarters of a mile out of Kilburn on the Thirsk Road there stands a house and some buildings on the roadside. A man lit his lantern and went out to tend a cow that was calving. Unfortunately a German plane was flying overhead and must have seen the light. A bomb was dropped in a field within a few hundred feet of the buildings. The ground was soggy and wet and the bomb sank into the earth before exploding. It left a massive hole and wet earth was flung all over the field. The man, beast and little beast were unharmed. I suppose a spell of wet weather can have its blessings.

Coming home from school one winter's evening I had to pass some large snowdrifts. On this particular evening I noticed a word marked out on one. It had four letters. I had never seen or heard this word and was puzzled. When I got home I asked Mam about it. I got a blast and was told, 'Never say that word again etc., etc.' Next day at school I asked my friends and a couple of boys and was soon informed. I gathered later it had been put there by prisoners of war working on the farm. Farmers certainly swore in those days but all I ever heard were b…….., blast and damn. *Never* the F word.

Just before the war an ice cream van sometimes came through the village. It arrived at playtime one afternoon. Mr. Clarke, the vicar, fancied one and was buying it, watched by two little infants. He must have felt sorry for them because he bought them one each. Word travels fast in such a situation and by the end of playtime half the school had been bought one (of course none of us ever had any money of our own). Mam said I should not have had one as vicars did not have much money.

Jack Moss. *Resident of Thirsk.*

As the storm clouds of war gathered Jack Moss's family, like all others, began their blackout preparations. In the Finkle Street cycle shop Jack's Dad was fined for showing a light which, it was claimed, might attract enemy aircraft. The police, at the time, patrolled the streets of Thirsk on foot, not only during the day but at night.

The war was only expected to last a year so Jack volunteered for the R.A.F as he didn't want to be conscripted into the army. Jack recalls the influx of the military, the requisitioning of buildings, the black marketing that was carried on from carts and cars in the Market Place and the building of concrete barriers to prevent enemy tanks using the roads. He also remembers the mock aerodrome at the top of Sutton Bank where wooden planes and flimsy sheds were built and landing lights installed to deceive the enemy. Jack recalls the water tank installed in the Market Place in case of fire and the barometer on the Clock Tower, coloured in weekly, encouraging the people to save.

During the war there was a shortage of batteries. To alleviate the problem Jack used to drive an Austin Seven van to Darlington where he would contact a supplier and hopefully stock up. Returning along Station Road, Thirsk, in the blackout with only the regulation van headlights showing, Jack hit something. What he had hit was a line of marching soldiers crossing the road. One soldier hit the bonnet, and the soldiers dragged the injured man into a house on Station Road. An ambulance came and the injured man was taken to the Lambert Hospital. Jack spent a sleepless night and was relieved when he learnt that the soldier was making a good recovery. Driving in the blackout was never much fun.

Jack returned to Thirsk during his spells of leave from the R.A.F. The pubs were increasingly busy and short of beer. One of the pubs he visited with a friend while on leave was the Old Three

> Thirsk Hockey team entertained a military team on Saturday. The result was a draw, the score being three goals each. To-day Thirsk team will entertain a strong side from Leeds University.

Tuns in Finkle Street. The landlord, recognising Jack, pulled him a pint but could not be persuaded to pull a pint for Jack's friend. During another spell of leave Jack met a Miss Parker who was not only the head-teacher of the Infants' School but the owner of a rather posh car - a Triumph Gloria. The car with its wire wheels, lock on hub caps, leather inflated seats as well as a Coventry Climax engine, was, in Jack's eyes, the ultimate car. Miss Parker had decided to lay the car up for the duration of the war for without petrol it was of little use. Jack, in conversation with her, asked if she was going to sell the Triumph. Her reply was, 'Yes, for £25.' Somehow Jack rustled up the money and on knocking on Miss Parker's door presented her with £25. Somewhat taken aback she kept her word and this was Jack's first car. When he came on leave he would smuggle a gallon of aviation fuel from the R.A.F. and mixing this with what petrol he could obtain he would enjoy a number of pleasurable motoring excursions.

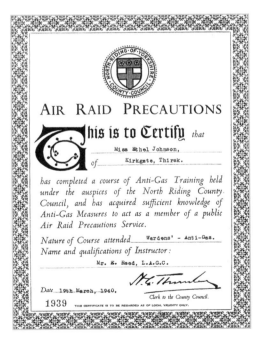

24th February 1941 (T.R.D.C.)
Letter from the Senior Staff Officer to the County Controller as follows:
A.R.P. (150) 20*th February, 1941.*
Dear Sir,

Sandbags. With reference to your request by telephone (through Mr.

Metcalfe, Sanitary Inspector), for a supply of sandbags to be distributed to householders in your area, the Regional Officer informs me that it is not considered that the provision of sand in Rural Areas is necessary - all that should be required would be for every householder to keep a bucket filled with earth together, if possible, with another filled with water, on each floor.

However I have approved the issue of 3,000 sandbags. Council will refund the cost to the County Council.

The present price of sandbags is £10 per thousand, i.e. £30 for 3,000.

Will you kindly acknowledge receipt of this letter and express your agreement to the above conditions.

> Yours faithfully
> J.Sewell
> Senior Staff Officer to the County Council.

Resolved that the Council purchase three thousand sandbags upon the above conditions of sale.

28th FEBRUARY 1941 (T.R.D.C.)

After general discussion on Fire Watching in the parishes of Thirsk and Sowerby it was recommended :

That it is essential that a watcher or a number of watchers should be continuously employed during hours when there is no-one astir. The Council suggests that a more definite definition of these hours should be prescribed black-out hours.

10th MARCH 1941 (T.R.D.C.)

A.R.P. sand for Fire Fighting: I beg to report that in the course of ordering sandbags to householders in the area as instructed it was found that the 3,000 sandbags requisitioned from the County were insufficient, and I had therefore to requisition another bale of 1,000 bags. There will probably be about 400 surplus. This work has been completed for the whole area. Besides delivering direct to householders in the village, filled bags were left at points in each village to be collected by outlying farmers etc.

I have had enquiries for the purchase of filled sandbags for fire fighting purposes for Clubs etc. in Thirsk and Sowerby and as there will probably be surplus filled bags I should be glad to know whether these could be sold.

Recommended that these be sold at 6d per bag delivered in Thirsk and Sowerby.

Letter from Mr. Jones stating that certain damage had been caused through alleged cutting off of the Thirkleby water supply and that he was holding the Council liable for such damage as no notice had been given that the water was being cut off.

Recommended that the Clerk reply informing Mr. Jones that the Thirkleby water supply had not been cut off, the cause of the failure of supply was a burst at Sutton water main over which the Council had no control.

Air Raid Shelters.

The Clerk submitted a report from Mr. Moore in regard to the provision of domestic or commercial shelters in certain parishes in the district, the estimated cost was £11,000.

Recommended that the matter be deferred until the Council meeting.

24th MARCH 1941 (T.R.D.C.)
Salvage - Village Dumps.

I have to report that the Scrap Iron Dump at Sessay appears to have been cleared without authority. I obtained certain information and, it is believed, the car number of the person who removed the material, and have reported the matter to the police. On receipt of full information I propose reporting to the Minister, Village Dumps Department for such action as they deem necessary.

Neil Graham.

Ted Atkinson, shoe repairer and Methodist, was, in 1937, one of the few people in Thirsk who ran a car. This he used to ferry Pastor George Graham and his family to their new home in South Terrace, Thirsk. A member of that family was a young boy - Neil Graham.

Neil's father was in Thirsk to take up his new post as Methodist Pastor in the town. The family quickly settled into their new environment and friends were made. Neil became an avid reader of the Yorkshire Post and Leeds Mercury and as a keen listener to the wireless realised that the country was heading for war. Neil's great pal in these pre-war years was Geoff Smith who lived at number one South Terrace. Both boys were excited at the prospect of war for they had seen the newsreels which clearly showed the devastation that would be caused by bombing. There would be wrecked houses to play in, bomb craters to hide in and plenty of material to build dens. The two lads, like all children, had little conception of the horrors of war.

Neil attended the British and Foreign School in Long Street which was a mile walk from his home. He came home for dinner but he had to agree with his teachers that 'he was not very good material for a schoolmaster to work with.' He became familiar with B. Smiths (the oldest established business in Great Britain), for his sister Mary worked there.

On the way back from chapel on 3rd September, 1939 Neil's family were told that the country was at war. A flurry of activity followed. Black-outs for windows were made as the public tried to follow regulation after regulation issued by the Government.

Thirsk began to fill with soldiers and there were rumours among the children of the town that schools would not open. The race-course became an army camp; buildings were requisitioned; gas masks had to be carried at all times and Neil's world seemed to turn upside down. The sound of marching feet and the noise of aircraft soon became part of everyday life. The few cars there were became even more dangerous to pedestrians. Car headlights were blacked out leaving only a narrow slit from which light could be projected to guide the motorist. The Sunday School room at the back of the Chapel in Thirsk became a meeting place for troops as they came into town. Here board games were available, coffee and tea served and facilities to write letters home provided. One person who attended not only the Chapel's Sunday School but was invited to the Graham's house for tea was Fred Weeks from Wales. Fred would later marry Neil's sister Mary.

In August the Graham family moved to Topcliffe. Here Neil attended Topcliffe School where Mr. W.G. Burton was head. Topcliffe village had its own defences, for Neil remembers that just over the bridge was a gun post made of hessian. Topcliffe had its own airfield as did Dishforth and Dalton. Those who crewed the planes became the new heroes of the young and not so young. Some of the soldiers and members of the R.A.F. and R.C.A.F. would, if possible, attend chapel services. After the normal evening service there would be another hour of hymn singing. The favourite hymn was 'The day thou gavest, Lord, is ending' and would compete with the noise of the aircraft.

Herbert Taylor, who ran the Post Office at Topcliffe, employed the young Neil Graham on a Saturday as a telegram boy. From nine in the morning until the office closed Neil would deliver telegrams to the surrounding aerodromes and villages. The former was an opportunity to cadge chewing gum and other delicacies from the Canadians who flew with Six Bomber Command. There seemed to be a constant noise of aircraft and Neil remembers his mother saying as the planes returned from a raid, 'Not many came back but they must have landed further south,' (a forlorn hope). His mother prepared umpteen teas and suppers for those in the services.

Once, during his time at Topcliffe, Neil fell in love with a girl in his class. To show her he really cared he saved his sweet coupons until he had enough for a bar of chocolate. On giving her the chocolate and expecting at least a hug all he got was a very down to earth, 'thank you.' As he now comments, 'Greater love hath no boy than this, that he gives up his sweet ration to the one he loved.' Neil had also managed to make a bogey. Even though it had buckled wheels it was used by Neil's friends to collect scrap tin and waste paper for the war effort. Neil recalls the great shire horses working on the farms, the horses and traps, the first tractors as technology slowly took a grip on agriculture. He didn't enjoy potato picking but quickly learned that some farmers were kinder to the pickers than others. Servicemen and women mingled freely with the village folk for all were united in a common cause. During 1941 to 1943 one of Neil's self imposed tasks was to keep a war diary. The diary, written in green, red and blue ink, includes cuttings from the Yorkshire Post and Leeds Mercury and in a neat hand lists Neil's account of wartime events, until he left the village to continue his education elsewhere.

14th APRIL 1941 (T.R.D.C.)

Recommended that the Austin car at present on hire from F. D. Todd and Sons, Thirsk, be purchased at a cost of £30 for use as a trailer unit for the Auxiliary Fire Service.

Recommended that the Fever Ambulance now used by the Northallerton R.D.C. be purchased for use as a trailer unit for the Auxiliary Fire Service at a cost of £20.

27th APRIL 1941
ATHENS CAPTURED BY THE GERMANS

8th MAY 1941 (diary)

Last night bombs were dropped half a mile from Topcliffe. This is the first time I have heard bombs drop since the war started.

12th MAY 1941 (diary)

Last night a lone enemy raider flew very low over Topcliffe and dropped three bombs half a mile away. I heard them drop and dad was out fire watching.

24th MAY 1941 (D/S)

One way streets for traffic.
Offenders fined at Thirsk.

The first case of failing to conform to the one way traffic signs in Thirsk came before the local Bench on Monday. The magistrates fined each of the four defendants five shillings.

13th JUNE 1941 (diary)

Last night we heard bombs drop on Topcliffe.

22nd JUNE 1941.
GERMANY INVADES RUSSIA

7th JULY 1941 (T.R.D.C.)

The Chairman drew the Committee's attention to the number of cases which were brought before the magistrates of people not observing the one way traffic rule at Finkle Street, and all those claimed that the necessary notices were not sufficient warning.

Recommended that the Council make representation to the Minister of Transport asking if more efficient signs could be erected.

14th JULY 1941 (T.R.D.C.)

Letter from the Thirsk District Water Company asking for permission to supply water to the R.A.F. station at Dalton.

Resolved that this be granted.

31st JULY 1941 (diary).

Last night a British plane crashed on Topcliffe aerodrome, all the crew were saved.

Margaret Josephs, (nee Burton). Resident of Thirsk.

Margaret, the daughter of Mr Burton, head-teacher of Topcliffe School, was attending a church service with her parents when war was declared on 3rd September 1939. The family were told the news by an aunt who had remained at home to listen to the Prime Minister Neville Chamberlain's broadcast. The church service at Topcliffe had been taken by the Rev. Chilman from Dalton for the congregation were waiting for a new Vicar.

The most urgent tasks, for which a certain amount of preparation had already been done, were now completed. Countless blackout curtains were made. All sewing of such curtains was done by hand for the family did not possess a sewing machine. These curtains were suspended on hooks screwed into the window frames. Windows were painted with a solution which it was hoped would prevent them shattering. Once applied the solution, when set, was difficult to remove, while those inside the house could not see clearly through the windows. Gas masks were issued and fitted and everyone was provided with an Identity Card. (Margaret's number was J.H.V.E. 17/4). Extra fire bricks, used to reduce the size of the fire, were put in place to conserve fuel.

The villagers quickly adapted to the changes that were taking place. Evacuees from the north-east arrived in the village and assembled in the big schoolroom while the billeting officer took them to their new abodes. Not only were the evacuees billeted but also the teachers who had accompanied them. The big schoolroom was to house three classes and three teachers while the small schoolroom accommodated the younger children.

Margaret was attending the Secondary School in Topcliffe Road, Thirsk, some four miles distant from the village. In September 1939 Mr. Peatfield, the head-teacher, decided that a number of zig-zag trenches should be dug in the grounds. The pupils, including the girls, provided the labour for the enterprise. The trenches were never used. Normal schooling did not resume for some time as once again evacuees had to be accommodated. Thirsk pupils attended the school in the mornings and then had lessons either at Church House or the Salem Chapel. When the new head was appointed, (Mr. Tillet), he arrived with loads of plums from his garden in Easingwold. Margaret and another pupil had to set to making plum jam to eke out school dinners. This batch of jam had to include the kernels from the plum stones and meant that every plum stone had to be broken open.

Miss Barker who taught Domestic Science and Needlework had volunteered to work at Northallerton Military Hospital and in May 1940 left to take charge of the catering. The hospital housed many veterans from the Dunkirk evacuation. The absence of Miss Barker resulted in Mr Tillet asking Margaret to take the classes and to keep the subject 'ticking over' until a new member of staff could be found. This proved a daunting task to the young girl from Topcliffe but for three days a week she took the cookery class while the

Gas-mask drill at Topcliffe, 1939. The war clouds gather again as Mr. W.G. Burton, headmaster, instructs his pupils in donning their civilian respirators. The cases slung on a string were standard issue

caretaker's wife did the other two days. School dinners were then nine pence per day.

Margaret's father was in the Local Defence Volunteers, (later the Home Guard), from the beginning. The church tower was used as an observation post. In early June 1944 the members of this organisation were in the schoolroom with rifles loaded with blank ammunition. During target practice one of the rifles went off and the bullet hit Mr. Burton who fell to the floor. Mr. Barningham applied a tourniquet to try and stop the bleeding while arrangements were made to take the injured man to Catterick Military Hospital. By all accounts it was a 'near run thing' for the headmaster.

The arrival of the cookery van is an event writ large in the memory of Margaret. Drawn by two horses it would arrive in the village and park outside the school-yard.

Initially it looked no larger than a gypsy caravan yet the first task of the driver, after tethering the horses, was to extend the van. This was done by winding out first one extension then another, thus doubling the size of the structure that was pulled by the horses, and sturdy legs would be put under the extensions to support them. Steps would be placed at the entrance, then two bags of coal would be ceremoniously dumped under the van. It was only then that the driver would return with his horses to his own village.

Next to arrive was Miss Sutherland who was in charge of the cookery van. On arrival at Topcliffe she found lodgings with Miss Jackson and her companion Miss Dowson at Beech House. One outbuilding was referred to as 'Woolworths' for here, in the outbuildings one might find that most essential item, a teapot to fit a broken teapot lid.

The girls in the leaving class at Topcliffe School had been anticipating the arrival of the cookery van. Those coming to school leaving age would be shown how and what to cook on a cooking range heated by the coals. The side boiler of the range had to be filled with water from the village water point. This water was carried by the girls in galvanised buckets.

Using non-rationed ingredients Miss Sutherland would demonstrate economical ways to prepare balanced meals. Recipes would be copied out as the ten or twelve pupils watched the demonstration. The pupils sitting on stools at scrubbed tables would be asked to help as the need arose.

Other sessions were involved with the washing and ironing of clothes and the cleaning of silver (borrowed from the headmaster). For the majority of the girls who attended it was an ideal opportunity to learn about their future, for the majority of girls would find employment in domestic service.

Sessions in the cookery van were either morning or afternoon and great store was set on having attended a session. The adult population was not

Fund raising at Topcliffe for 'Salute the Soldier' drive

neglected during the war, for Miss Sutherland would provide classes in the evening for them.

At the end of three weeks a driver and two horses would be hired and the cookery van would go slowly to its next venue.

Recipes used at the evening class which my friend, Jean Dickenson, and I attended :-

Scotch Broth

2 quarts stock or water.
Any scraps of mutton.
2 teaspoons finely chopped parsley.
2 ounces pearl barley.
2 carrots.
2 small onions
2 leeks.
(Peas beans etc.).

Dumplings

3 ounces of flour.
1 ounce of suet.
½ teaspoon of baking powder (small)
Pinch salt.
Cold water.
Herbs, parsley, or chopped onion.

Sausage and tomato pie.

8 ounces flour.
Pinch salt.
Cold water to mix to a stiff paste.
3 ounces fat (lard and margarine mixed).
½ teaspoon baking powder.
1lb sausages.
½ lb tomatoes.

Swiss apple tart.

½ lb short pastry.
1 lb apples.
4 tablespoons syrup.
½ pint thick custard.
½ teasp. grated nutmeg.
Rind and juice of a lemon.

Method

Stew apples in syrup
Add lemon juice
Beat well, add rind and nutmeg
Mix with custard
Hot oven for ½ hour

Fish pie.

1lb smoked haddock.
½ pint milk.
½ oz. flour.
2lbs. mashed potatoes.
Pepper
browned bread crumbs.

Simmer fillets in milk, make sauce, put flaked fish in dish, sauce and potatoes, crumbs on top, brown and heat through.

Leisure activities for Margaret centred round the church and the school. The odd visit to the cinema in Thirsk meant a stay overnight with a school friend. Using a torch with the glass covered in cellophane with a slit allowing the light to penetrate the darkness meant night outings were infrequent. Potato picking, digging for victory, bottling fruit went hand in hand with knitting comforts for the troops.

The gypsies continued their visits to Topcliffe and camped by the bridge. Dr. Mitchell would walk down to welcome them. Dances were organised for service personnel in the big room at the school. This was never very satisfactory for the desks were removed and stored outside where they were frequently rained on.

'Salute The Soldier' and 'Wings For Victory' weeks were held and the targets set often exceeded. During the war the Women's Institute organised a mock 'Village Wedding.' Many authentic old clothes were worn and a cardboard cake prepared. A number of Institute members dressed up as men and the Wedding procession paraded round the village. The Toll Booth at Topcliffe became the Y.M.C.A. for Topcliffe,

Dalton and Skipton aerodromes. The manageress was a Mrs Caffrey who was helped by volunteers. Margaret and her mother and aunt did one night each week at the Y.M.C.A. Here all nationalities could assemble for tea, sandwiches and a chat. A record was set one night when Margaret poached sixty eggs and toasted sixty slices of bread using only a small battered pan and a single toaster.

Margaret was a participant in the government's drive to 'Make do and Mend' and to make 'Something New out of Something Old.' Margaret needed a new skirt when she went to college, and her mother suggested that she should try to alter a suit belonging to her brother which was hanging in the wardrobe.

Her brother no longer lived at home so Margaret set to and unpicked the trousers and turned the pieces - using the inside as the outside to make a four-gored skirt. The exercise was successful and the skirt was worn for a very long time.

The sequel to this was when Margaret's brother came to stay for Christmas and went to get his suit saying it would be useful when fire watching. Instead of her brother going for the suit, Margaret's mother told

Margaret to go. Margaret put on the skirt and offered it to her brother Glynn for fire watching.

Afterwards Margaret's mother admitted that she had been at the bottom of all of this for she knew that her son hadn't wanted the suit for fire watching, or anything else. However, all this saved much needed clothing coupons.

The sound of aeroplane engines was never far from Margaret's life. Sometimes the noise emanated from enemy aircraft and when bombs were dropped the dining room table provided the only shelter. In 1942 Margaret went to train as a teacher at Ripon Training College where she and other students continued to dig for victory and knit.

22nd SEPTEMBEr 1941 (T.R.D.C.)

Salvage:- It is estimated that sales from the Salvage campaign total approximately £190 to date.

Letter from the Regional Officer stating that owing to the urgent demand for labour it was not proposed to sanction erection of shelters in 'C' areas at the present time and as the Council has been scheduled as a 'C' area the shelters would not be proceeded with.

4th OCTOBER 1941 (diary).

Yesterday the King and Mr. Churchill passed through Thirsk after inspecting troops outside Thirsk.

8th OCTOBER 1941 (diary). On Sunday night Topcliffe was filled with Scottish soldiers after wide scale manoeuvres with the Home Guard.

3rd NOVEMBER 1941 (T.R.D.C.)

Unnecessary Railings Survey. The members of the Sub-Committee met on Wednesday, 22nd October and railings were viewed in Thirsk and Sowerby. On Wednesday 29th October the Sub-Committee, with the exception of Mr. Lambert, viewed railings at Carlton Miniott, Sandhutton, Skipton-on-Swale, Holme-on-Swale, Ainderby Quernhow, Sinderby, Pickhill and Catton. Practically the whole of the railings in Thirsk and Sowerby were scheduled for removal irrespective of whether they were on boundary walls or only on low copings, the view being taken that the railings were protecting nothing of importance other than gardens or areas at the front of houses.

It is, however, my opinion that the removal of railings from low copings or walls will cause a danger during black-out hours, as there will be some risk of pedestrians tripping over the coping obstruction and injuring themselves. Also the railings will probably be replaced by some other form of material in order to give the accustomed privacy to the houses.

In view of further inspection of railings in the area it would be helpful if some advice could be given on this matter.

Ministry of Food Store: a site plan has been submitted showing site of proposed warehouse on Station Road, Thirsk.

8th November 1941 (diary).
Last night we heard bombs at Topcliffe falling some distance away. Other bombs fell on four north-east towns.

2nd December 1941
CONSCRIPTION FOR WOMEN
Unmarried women between the ages of 20 and 30 were to be called up.

7th December 1941
JAPAN ATTACKS PEARL HARBOUR
On Sunday 7th December Japanese fighters and bombers attacked American ships lying at Pearl Harbour. Airfields were also attacked. Some 2,330 Americans were left dead or dying.

7th December 1941
AMERICA DECLARED WAR ON JAPAN
Roosevelt, President of the United States of America, declared in a message to Congress that 'the United States of America was suddenly and deliberately attacked by naval and air forces of the Empire of Japan'. He added, 'No matter how long it may take us to overcome this premeditated invasion, the American people in their righteous might will win through to absolute victory.'

8th December 1941
WAR DECLARED ON JAPAN BY WINSTON CHURCHILL
Japanese troops invaded Malaya and Winston Churchill, Prime Minister, informed the Japanese Government 'that a state of war exists between our two countries.'

8th December 1941 (T.R.D.C.)
Application has been made for a supply of sandbags for fire prevention services at the Agricultural Hostel, Kilvington Road, Thirsk. I have arranged for same.
Recommended that same be agreed to.

11th December 1941
GERMANY DECLARES WAR ON
UNITED STATES OF AMERICA
The war has now become a global war. Also by this date the retreat of the German army from Moscow had begun.

25th December 1941
HONG KONG SURRENDERS

Hong Kong was the first British possession to fall to Japan. Some 11,000 British soldiers were taken prisoner.

James Burns. *Resident of Thirsk.*

In late May and early June 1940 Jim, who lived in Topcliffe, was carrot weeding for a local farmer, a Mr. Robinson. This was the period of Dunkirk when thousands of troops were evacuated from the beaches of this French town. Jim recalls the quiet voices of the grown-ups as they discussed the implications of the event. An air of gloom and despondency seemed to settle over the village. This did not last, for the village was to be turned upside down with the arrival of the military and civilian contractors. The farms of Wilkinson, Kays and Masterman were demolished as the airfields were constructed.

The Government had already prepared the population of the country for some of the impact of war. Gas masks had been issued and fitted, a Local Defence Volunteer Force, (later the Home Guard), had been hastily organised. The boys in Topcliffe were fascinated by this organisation for the men involved used to practise their drill and marching techniques in the village. One of the older boys called Horace Webster decided to have his own platoon of boy soldiers. He persuaded a number of other lads to join him. Broom handles and sticks were the weapons used as Horace marched the platoon up and down aping their elders. Jim says, 'It didn't last long. We learnt more sense.'

Topcliffe was home to two hotels, The Angel and the Black Bull, and an inn, the White Swan. There were also several shops - the cycle shop, the tea room run by the Thomases, Barningham's General Stores, Hardy's Store, a fish shop run by Bentalls and a Post Office and General Store operated by Mr. Taylor. Jim and his friend Cyril Bowen used to borrow 'The War Illustrated' from Liza Allenby.

This was a magazine they could not afford so Liza Allenby used to let them 'borrow it'. Taken to school it was read quickly and surreptitiously under the desk lid before being returned to its rightful owner.

School life at the beginning of the war was disrupted by the war's very uncertainty. For a short period of time schools were closed and then re-opened part-time.

Windows were criss-crossed with brown tape and Mr. Burton, headmaster, gave the pupils drill based on his experiences of the 1914-18 war. Not only did the pupils perform drill but Mr. Burton would suddenly shout, 'Gas attack!' and they would scurry to put on their gas masks. Evacuees from Sunderland and Gateshead schools began to arrive in the village with their teachers. These additional pupils simply added to the life of the village where they were billeted. The schoolrooms were used for lectures by the military and for dances. It was the schoolboys who moved the desks to enable these events to take place. Mr. Burton became a sergeant in the Home Guard and was accidentally shot during a lecture on rifles. He was hospitalised and absent from school for some time.

As the war settled into an uneasy pattern local men and women would disappear as conscription made its inroads. They would re-appear on leave and cause great excitement among the boys in the village. The wireless became the main focus of news. Jim's brother managed to find a map of Europe and mapped the progress of the war. Jim and his brother also used to listen to Lord Haw-Haw broadcasting German propaganda and then try to imitate his voice with the words, 'Germany calling, Germany calling'.

Slowly the aerodromes around Topcliffe became operational. Different sounds could now be heard. The aircraft machine guns would be tested as well as the engines of the planes. Crashes were numerous and somehow or other the boys of the village got to know where. A furious bike ride would then follow for whoever got there first got first choice of souvenirs. Live bullets, shrapnel and perspex were prize possessions among the young. The live bullets were collected for their cordite and when enough was gathered would be set on fire. The boys would then wait for the explosion. Those bullets they didn't use were buried in the garden for another day.

One boy put a live bullet in the stove in the classlroom. Fortunately the damage was slight. Sometimes an aircraft would catch fire as Jim and his friends rushed to the scene. On one occasion they found a flying boot with a severed leg inside.

Watching the planes take off occupied a lot of leisure time. Jim and his friends would cycle to Dishforth Airfield, alongside the Great North Road. Whitley bombers were dispersed on the opposite side. As the planes taxied across the road the pilots would wave at the boys and the rear gunner would waggle his machine guns. 'This, to us lads, was excitement beyond compare as we watched them take off a few feet above our heads,' says Jim. Jim's relationship with the R.A.F. grew more familiar when he became a telegram boy on a Saturday. His role was to take telegrams to Dalton, Dishforth or Topcliffe airfields. These he would deliver to the guardroom. During one such delivery he saw his first black man - a Sergeant Pilot. Jim could hardly believe his eyes for he believed, along with many of his friends, that black men were uneducated and here was one who was a pilot! Jim and his friends used to crawl under the fencing surrounding the airfield and talk to the crews before take off. All the boys who did this would promise to introduce the aircrew to their sisters if they would only take them on a bombing mission. Once the boys were caught and given a real dressing down in the guardroom. Not a pleasant experience. On another occasion Jim was given a pair of wings which he persuaded his mother to sew on his jumper. He remembers how proud he felt.

Aircrew were not the only servicemen in the surrounding area. The army also had a base known as the 'Mob' in Station Road. These khaki clad men were part of R.E.M.E., responsible for the tanks and Bren gun carriers that trundled through the village. There were also anti-aircraft and search light units stationed nearby to defend the airfield. On one occasion a large convoy of army personnel arrived and camped in local fields. The villagers made them welcome and provided tea and food.

A number of villagers took in the wives of service personnel. Jim's mother was one of these. She welcomed the wife of Sergeant Pears who was a wireless operator and air gunner. Great sadness descended on the Burns household when he failed to return home from an operation over enemy territory. Eventually Mrs. Pears' parents came and collected her. Jim's mother also did a great deal of washing for the aircrew and the family really got to know them. One day there was a knock at the door asking for the men's washing. When asked why they did not collect it themselves the reply was that they had been killed on an operation. Another great period of sadness.

Jim collected sweet Caporal Cigarette packets from the aircrew. These packets contained silhouettes of aircraft and helped Jim's recognition skills. A number of personnel were based at Skellfield School. These were R.C.A.F./R.A.F. aircrew and often the Wellington bombers would 'beat up' the school. One Halifax pilot had a habit of buzzing his girl friend's farmhouse. Neighbouring farmers were furious as such behaviour caused the farm animals to stampede and pregnant animals to abort.

Jim continued to work part-time. Papers were delivered to various households except on Sundays. He also helped to milk Herbert Barningham's cows. Sugar beet was hoed, carrots weeded, corn stooked and potatoes harvested. During the potato harvest buckets were not provided and Jim took either a galvanised or enamel bucket. Once the farmer left Jim in charge of the tractor during the potato harvest. As he spun the potatoes out of the ground they were supposed to be gathered by Land Army girls and some soldiers. Little was harvested as the girls and the soldiers kept 'disappearing'. Not only was there farm work to do but the vegetable garden at home to be cultivated. These vegetables were necessary for the family's well-being.

It was not all work. During the hot summers swimming in the River Swale would be enjoyed. The annual Chapel outing was another event Jim looked forward to. During the war this was to Reeth.

There was no air raid shelter at the Burns' household. When the siren went it was a case of under the stairs or under the dining room table. Neither were very comfortable. The Germans made several raids on the airfields and the noise of the bombs as they exploded could be heard for miles. Allied and German aircrew were buried in local cemeteries. Jim recalls watching the

12 Platoon 'C' Company Homeguard - Topcliffe, 25th December 1941
  Photograph taken on lawn at Angel Hotel, Topcliffe
Back Row : G Hunter, F Langstaff,————, M Ormston, J Mackie, N Jackson,
G Garbutt, P Yeadon, B Bowen
Middle Row : ————, ————, H Hodgson, F Fothergill, B Wade, B Thompson,
L Jackson, J Bell, J Rayner, B Ward
Front Row : A Ormston, J Grainger, J R Bumby, T Gatenby, H Pollington,
W Sigsworth, E Barningham, T Bell, B Henderson, A Egan.

impressive ceremony as a member of aircrew was laid to rest with full military honours.

Servicemen were noted for pinching bikes and dumping them once they arrived at their destination. One local woman did not know her bike was missing until she saw a Canadian airman riding past her. Only then she realised it was her bike. Jim delivered groceries to the local farms. He was terrified when cycling down Cundall Road with its tall trees, high hedges and narrow road. It felt really 'spooky'. Occasionally when the gypsies came to the village fights would break out between them and the Canadians. One of the treats for the village children was being able to attend the cinema at Topcliffe Camp. Here the latest films could be seen as well as images of the war on a newsreel.

When the Italian and German prisoners of war first appeared in the village they were not supposed to talk to the villagers. However barriers were soon broken down as people grew used to seeing them with their identifying patches on their clothes. A football match was arranged between the German

Topcliffe Homeguard undergoing training, 25th December 1945
Standing : P Yeadon, J R Bumby, W Sigsworth, B Bowen, H Pollington
E Barningham
On lawn : ———, ———, B Henderson, ———, B Thompson, L Jackson, B Ward

prisoners of war and an England team recruited from the village. The match took place at Thirkleby P.O.W. camp and Jim remembers a German saying, 'Every time they had a corner it would be half a goal,' - it was the only English he knew. Jim thinks they lost the match but he has a vivid memory of food he had not seen for years.

Jim was also a keen stamp collector and was so excited when a member of aircrew promised to bring him a Scottish stamp.

Throughout 1941, 1942 and 1943 the airfields around Topcliffe were spasmodically attacked by German aircraft. The odd air battle would be witnessed as fighters engaged the enemy.

Jim remembers the early war years as being the most exciting time of his life. His most impressive memory is the assembly of a bomber force over the Vale of York preparing for raids on Germany. The thunderous roar of the engines seemed to go on for ever as the planes gathered. This was followed by an eerie silence as they headed for the North Sea.

From 1943 to 1945 Jim lived with some Chapel friends in Northamptonshire.

29th December 1941 (T.R.D.C.)

The Chairman mentioned that appeals had been made in an effort to reduce the number of road deaths, and after discussion it was resolved that the County Council be urged to provide 'cat's eye' pads for pedestrian crossings wherever practical.

CHAPTER SIX
1942-1943

5th JANUARY 1942 (T.R.D.C.)
Fire Brigade and Air Raid Precautions Committee.
Recommended

That a Fire Guard Staff Officer be appointed at a salary of £3 per week to work under the Home Civil Defence Officer and the question of payment of travelling   expenses be left to the Home Civil Defence Officer

That 61 stirrup pumps be applied for.

That 550 civilian steel helmets be applied for.

10th JANUARY 1942 (diary)

To-day started to collect salvage in Topcliffe. We did this so that old tins could be melted down and remade.

12th JANUARY 1942 (T.R.D.C.)
Sanitary, Housing and Planning Committee.

Salvage: As referred to at the council meeting I have now purchased approximately 37 dozen sacks at 5/- doz. for Salvage Work. Many of these have already been distributed to the village dumps of which I now have 43 arranged, besides 5 in Thirsk and Sowerby for the Boy Scouts collections. The Scouts are doing their best, but their numbers are few and unless they get the promised assistance of children I shall be obliged to make a special collection this month to ensure no promises are missed.

Waste Paper Contest 1942 (January.)

The above contest resulted in a total of 28 tons of Waste Paper and books being collected from the areas of Thirsk and Wath Council during January which is equal approximately two tons per 1,000 of the population

31st JANUARY 1942
JAPANESE INVADE BURMA

8th FEBRUARY 1942 (diary)

From today soap will be rationed.

This was to save shipping space. From Monday 7th February soap may be bought only against a coupon or buying permit. The oils and fats used in soap manufacture occupy much shipping space and some of this must be saved for food. You will have four coupons in each four-weekly period, and will be able to use these how and when you like within the period. There will be no registration and you may buy from any shop stocking the kind you require.

Each of the four coupons will enable you to buy any one of the following:-

either 4ozs hand soap (common household soap)

or 3 ozs toilet soap.

or 6ozs soap powder No.1.

or 12ozs soap powder No.2.

or 6ozs soft soap.

Rationing will not apply to shaving soaps, dental soaps, shampoo powders, liquid soap or scourers.

15th FEBRUARY 1942

SINGAPORE FALLS
62,000 INDIAN, AUSTRALIAN, BRITISH TAKEN AS PRISONERS

Four days after the surrender of Singapore, Japanese planes bombed Darwin, Australia.

25th MARCH 1942 (diary)

King and Queen passed through Topcliffe on their way to inspect the 'drome. This is the first time in my life I have seen royalty.

29th APRIL 1942 (diary)

Last night enemy aircraft raided York. We heard the bombs at Topcliffe and were all up. Five of the raiders were destroyed.

4th MAY 1942 (T.R.D.C.)

Fuel Rationing: In view of the proposed Fuel Rationing Scheme a register of all purchasers of coal in the Council's area is under preparation.

1st JUNE 1942 (T.R.D.C)
Medical Officer's Report.

The Medical Officer attended and reported on the health of the district and instructions were given as to the procedure for the immunisation of children against diphtheria. He also reported that the ambulance which the council have placed at his disposal for use as an Air Raid Precautions Ambulance was useless.

MINISTRY OF FOOD

SOAP
RATIONING

FROM MONDAY, FEBRUARY 9TH, soap may be bought only against a coupon or buying permit. The oils and fats used in soap manufacture occupy much shipping space, and some of this must be saved for food. You will have 4 coupons in each 4-weekly period, and will be able to use these how and when you like within the period. There will be no registration, and you may buy from any shop stocking the kind you require.

Each of the four coupons which make up a four-weeks' ration will entitle you to any one of the following :—
- either 4 ozs. Hard Soap (common Household Soap in bars or pieces)
- or 3 ozs. Toilet Soap
- or 3 ozs. Soap Flakes or Chips
- or 6 ozs. Soap Powder No. 1
- or 12 ozs. Soap Powder No. 2
- or 6 ozs. Soft Soap.

Rationing will not apply to shaving soaps or dental soaps, shampoo powders, liquid soap, or scourers.

The coupons to be used are those in the frame at the top of Page 15 of the YELLOW BOOK (RB 9)—the book you use for jam. Coupon numbers and periods will be the same as for sugar and tea, so that you will start with coupons 29 to 32 for the first period—February 9th to March 8th. Coupons 1-28 are of no value.

Coupons will not be cut out, but must be cancelled by the shopkeeper in ink or indelible pencil.

¶ MEMBERS OF THE SERVICES, ETC.
Holders of the Services Registration Card (RB 8 X) will use the frame of coupons at the bottom of page 4. Holders of Leave or Duty Ration Cards (RB 8) will use the coupons marked " Y " on page 3. Special coupons will be issued to other members of the services. Weekly Seamen holding Ration Book RB 6 will use the coupons marked " A " on the last green page (leaf 11).

¶ TRAVELLERS
Persons who have been granted travellers' facilities will use the frame of coupons at the top of Form RT 2 inserted in their ration books.

¶ ESTABLISHMENTS AND BUSINESS USERS
Residential establishments will use the Yellow Ration Books of their residents, as they do for rationed foods. Public Authorities and Business users must ask the local Food Office for a Permit application Form. This covers institutions, catering establishments, shops, offices, and factories which buy soap for washrooms and cleaning, textile manufacturers, and also such concerns as laundries and those who regularly take in washing.

TO WHOLESALERS AND RETAILERS OF SOAP
No further sales of soap must be made to consumers except against a coupon or buying permit. Ask your Food Office for a copy of Soap Instructions No. 1 and No. 2 (for retailers only) which contain full trade instructions.

Shopkeepers are reminded that they must cancel coupons in ink or indelible pencil, starting with No. 29.

6ᵗʰ JUNE 1942 (D/S)
Woman on Careless Talk Charge.

Raid Plans and Movements Discussed. Charged under the Defence Regulations with having communicated to other persons information appertaining to aircraft operations, personnel, crashes and casualties which might directly or indirectly have been of use to the enemy.

7ᵗʰ JUNE 1942

DEATH CAMP KILLINGS INSIDE GERMAN OCCUPIED POLAND BECOME PUBLIC KNOWLEDGE

21ˢᵗ JUNE 1942

TOBRUK FALLS

Some 30,000 troops surrendered to the German General Rommel.

6ᵗʰ July 1942 (T.R.D.C.)

Proposed Camp for Forestry Workers.

Application has been made on behalf of the Ministry of Supply for your approval in writing for the erection of Tarran Huts at Boltby for housing Forestry workers. No plans available.

Recommended that this given subject to satisfactory sanitation.

Edna Garbutt, *(nee Dancy)*.

Edna Garbutt who lived with her granny in Middles-brough became, for a time, a conductress with United Buses. While out with her friends one of the places they passed was the recruitment office of 'The Women's Land Army'. Attracted by the posters inviting young girls to work on the land Edna and her friends dared one another to enter the office and sign up. Edna was one of those who dared and duly signed the necessary papers. Thinking little would come of it Edna continued her life as usual.

However, some three weeks after signing up, parcels were delivered at the house, an unusual event in itself. .Opening these Edna discovered that they contained her Land Army uniform including the Boy Scout type hat. Somewhat shocked at the rapid turn of events Edna and her friend Margaret Burrows were issued with rail warrants and ordered to report to the Land Army lady at Thirsk station.

On arriving in Thirsk Edna was taken from the station to the Land Army Hostel in Stockton Road. This Hostel was situated some distance from the huts in which soldiers were stationed. Edna describes these soldiers as a 'blooming nuisance' as they were always pestering the young Land Army girls.

The warden at the Hostel was a Mrs. Keith, 'a lovely woman,' who had a daft boxer dog as a pet. The Hostel comprised a large room which acted as a dormitory, two further rooms, while the warden had her own rooms. There were also bathrooms and a dining room. The hut was heated by coke stoves but always seemed cold. The girls were expected to help in the kitchen, with the cleaning, and to do their own laundry. A mangle was provided and on one occasion a girl decided to dry her hair in it. Unfortunately the girl's hair became entangled in the machine and the only way to release her was by cutting her hair. An unpleasant experience.

Edna had been issued with two sets of overalls, one to wear and one in the wash. Reveille was at six in the morning. In the beginning an agricultural van would collect the girls for work and deliver them to the outlying farms. Edna had no experience of rural life and hid from her first cow. As she and the other Land Girls became accustomed to farm work she found she loved the outdoor life. As they became more experienced the girls were issued with bikes and on these, with a lunch box strapped on the back of the bike, set off for work under their own power.

Jobs undertaken were potato picking, when 10d a day extra was paid, snagging turnips, bottling milk at Fowler-Jones farm, and threshing. Edna used to find threshing a nightmare. She hated the noise of the thresher. Different farms had different implements. A number still had working horses, others were more mechanised. At allowance

(break) time some farmers provided a drink and a bite to eat - others provided nothing. On one occasion Edna was invited to sit at the farmer's table with the men. However when the farmer, at one end of the table, and his wife at the other , took their false teeth out and put them on the table Edna found it disgusting and retreated to the barn. On another occasion, while working at Stokesley, a farm worker had, as a joke, slipped a litter of mice into her pocket. Edna says she nearly died when she put her hand in her pocket and felt the mice wriggling about.

Normally the girls worked five and a half days a week and finished about five o'clock. Leisure, when not too tired, meant a visit to the Y.M.C.A. in Castlegate where chocolate could be bought and comics and papers could be read. Sometimes a week-end would be spent at home. Should they stay in Thirsk, then it generally meant working on the land. Money was scarce. Some was spent on an odd visit to the cinema where Edna would watch the stars weave their magic. Money was also spent on mending materials, soap and the odd treat. One of Edna's pleasures was attending All Saints Church and enjoying the facilities the members of the church provided. Very occasionally Edna and her friends would visit the snug in the White Horse pub on the corner of Stammergate and Long Street. The girls would have a game of darts and put a sign on the door 'No men allowed'. The landlady, who knew nothing of this, was not best pleased.

Edna, who had to hand in her uniform at the end of the war, stayed in Thirsk and married a local man.

11th July 1942
James Severs.

James lived with his family at 49, Station Road, Thirsk, in a house built by his father Jack. During the war the race course was turned into an army barracks and after one particular air raid James remembers walking to school and watching soldiers drag out blood-stained mattresses after a direct hit on the barracks.

James' best friend was Adam Rose and on the 11th July, 1942, 'while out cycling in our oldest clothes, both of us spotted a cloud of black smoke down Station Road.' James jokingly said to Adam, 'Hey, your house is on fire.' They pedalled furiously towards the smoke to find that a Halifax bomber had sheared off the top storey of James' house and the other semis, and was straddled right across the road.

'My father was in the front room working on some plans and my sister June was on the toilet at the back. He managed to save her and himself, unhurt.'

The crash caused major problems for the Severs family as they had nowhere to live. James' father, mother and sister went to live with his father's business partner but there was no room for James who was eventually billeted with old Mr. Rayner who was a Chapel going friend of his mother's.

CRASH ON STATION ROAD (E.A.M.)
HALIFAX MARK 2.

Crashed into house on Station Road after doing an overshoot at Topcliffe, 16.20 hours. Cause not known. Four of the crew slightly hurt. Aircraft's nose nudged the race course fence.

Houses damaged:

No. 43. Knowles - damaged - repaired.

No.45. Mrs. Harriet Eden - out when it happened. Took roof off.

No.47. Cawoods occupied.

No. 49. Severs family - beyond repair.

11th July 1942 (E.A.M.)

Spitfire, Mark 5 crashed and burnt near Topcliffe /Thirsk Road. Pilot killed.

Chris Wright. *Resident of Thirsk.*

While Chris's father was on war service in the army his wife helped to run the Wright's news agency business in Thirsk.

Mrs Wright was given privileges not meted out to many civilians during the war. Granny Wright drove a Morris 10 while Chris's parents had a Morris 8. During the war you were allowed to keep your car provided you removed the wheels and distributor cap. Mum was allowed petrol coupons which gave her just enough fuel to get her to and from the aerodrome each day. Once there she was permitted to drive in all areas and Officers' Messes to sell

```
                                No.60 Maintenance Unit,
                                Royal Air Force,
                                Shipton-by-Beningbrough,
Ref: 60MU/304/Accts/R.9419.           Y O R K.

                                8th October, 1942.

Dear Madam,
                Aircraft accident at Station Road,
            Thirsk, on 11th July, 1942.
        -------------------------------

        Receipt of your letter dated 8th October, 1942
is acknowledged with thanks.

        It is understood that Messrs. Westwick & Co. have
the repair work in hand.  As the owner of the property,
and the individual from whom a Satisfaction Note will ultimately
be required, you are fully entitled to request full details of
the position from the builders direct.

        Should you incur, quite unavoidably, extra expenses
by the storage of furniture and rental of alternative
accomodation, Air Ministry will give favourable consideration
to any claim for net out-of-pocket expenses up till the date
that your house is fit for re-occupation.

        Any such claim may well be considered when the
repair work is complete.  Meanwhile, it is suggested that you
notify this Unit officially if it is your intention to apply
for reimbursement of these expenses later.

        Finally it is pointed out that should you desire
an advance of money to cover immediate expenses, application
on your behalf will readily be made by this Unit.  If this
course will help to relieve the financial burden, please notify
the Damage Officer.

        Certified statements showing how much you have been
called upon to pay for alternative accomodation and for
furniture storage will be of value to support any application
furnished to Headquarters.

                Yours faithfully,

                [signature]

                    Flight Lieutenant,
                for Squadron Leader
                Commanding No.60(M) Unit.

Mrs. H. Eden,
59 Station Road,
THIRSK,
Yorks.
```

newspapers. She could have gone anywhere and was never challenged.

The journey there and back each day was no picnic either. If the car would start she had to drive with hooded headlights no matter what the weather, thick fog, snow etc. All the white lines and signposts had been removed in case the Germans invaded and there were no street lights. Black-out curtains - those thick grey blankets - had to be hung over every window and each night someone would patrol the streets to make sure there was not a slit of light showing anywhere in the town. At night you could use a flashlight, (torch), with a small covered beam directed downwards for if there was so much as a pin prick of light, the Jerries would, according to Mum, drop a stick of bombs.

The car frequently wouldn't start and Mum had to get someone to crank the car using a cranking handle. To get the newspapers from the Railway Station to the shop every morning Mum would haul them on to a trolley, haul the trolley over the railway lines and load the car. If the car wouldn't start the trolley was pushed over a mile to the shop.

There were aerodromes at Skipton-on-Swale, Dalton, Dishforth and Topcliffe. They could only turn one lot of landing lights on at a time as Jerry planes were always waiting to strike. Mum said you could tell the enemy planes by the difference in engine noise. One time when she went to Dalton aerodrome the thin walls were full of holes. When she asked what had happened, she was told they had had a bombing raid. One of Mum's customers had been killed outright as she sat at her desk. Mum often spoke of the wonderful young airmen who disappeared overnight and were never seen again. During the Cologne bombing raids half the squadron was wiped out. One day Mum managed to get one packet of cigarettes from Granny Wright, who used to save a 10 pack for her favourite lady customers, and for one of her airmen who didn't come back from a raid that day.

Whenever the air raid sirens went Chris would be put in his carry basket under the dining table with both drop leaves down to protect him. His Mum said she had a knife ready to kill him if need be. Thankfully the only incident to affect the family was when a British bomber landed on top of his Nana's semi-detached house in Station Road. The Cawood/Severs half next door was demolished whilst the nose of the plane was parked on his Nana's half and his mum's bedroom was destroyed when the wing had

caught it. When told that a plane had crashed on the house they immediately drove out to see if everyone was all right. But they were stopped by a roadblock and not allowed through. They left the car and cut across the fields behind the house on foot. His Mum spotted his Nana's white hair and said, 'Oh thank goodness, Mother's O.K.' Chris's Mum went back to work the next day and asked who had parked their plane on her Mum's house only to be greeted by silence. Much later his mother gave an airman a lift to the Station and he let on that he had been part of the crew. All of them survived the crash. The damage to the house was considerable. Live ammunition was dug out of the garden for years after the crash.

13th July 1942 (T.R.D.C.)

Letter from Mrs. M.A. Davies asking if the boardroom could be available for a series of five refresher Anti-Gas lectures to be held on Thursday evenings. The Thirsk Market Place Fire Watchers suggested that the equipment bought by them at a cost £3.3s.0d should be purchased by the Council as the Scheme was now under the direction of the Assistant Fire Guard Staff Officer and it was recommended that the Council purchase the equipment at the original cost of £3.3s.0d.

Norah Foster. *Evacuated to Thirsk.*

It was the second evacuation for Gateshead Grammar School. At the beginning of the war we were evacuated to Bishop Auckland for about two terms. Everyone gradually drifted back home so the school eventually re-opened. When the Germans invaded Norway it was thought that the north-east might be blitzed so, in the early summer holidays we were sent away again. As the school was about six hundred strong it was split in half. Some, the science specialists, went to Yorebridge Grammar and our half, mainly the Arts specialists, went to Thirsk.

I don't remember the journey, by train I think, but I remember being left till last! I had been left off the list apparently and I felt very sick and homesick and lonely sitting on my own. In the end I was taken to a billet in a terrace off Station Road where a younger girl was already installed. It was the house of an elderly spinster and it was not a happy place. It was gloomy, repressive and rather hungry. The girl next door was very kind to us. She was about my age (16), and lived with her widower father.

As it was summer we were not required to go to school at first. The weather was good, and we did a lot of exploring around Thirsk and its surroundings. Transport was practically non-existent. The market was full of farm produce and such goods as plums, apples etc. were extremely cheap.

My sister had passed the eleven plus exam so I thought we should be billeted together. Two sixth formers were leaving and they suggested the lady at their billet would have us. She didn't want little ones as she had a pre-school child herself, so I visited her in Stockton Road. It was a very pleasant billet as she was only in her mid-twenties, although her husband was a few years older. On the whole it was a friendly place and we were convenient baby-sitters. I'll call her Brenda, which was not her real name.

They moved away later and until a few years back we exchanged cards every Christmas, and a school friend and I went a couple of times for a week-end after we left school. I think she must have died as the cards suddenly stopped.

At first we went to school half time as Thirsk Grammar School had the premises in the morning but later halls were used for morning school. We sixth formers were in Church House and we often spent break times watching Alf Wight and 'Siegfried' go in and out. There was only one boy in the Arts Sixth and he couldn't stand it so he went home. My sister, in first year, had morning lessons in Ebenezer, (Salem) Chapel in Finkle Street.

We never seemed to have much to do with Thirsk School, either staff or pupils, but we older girls got to know some of the sixth form boys. There were groups of us in the Market Place and a bit of harmless flirting, but nothing serious.

The place was full of soldiers living in various halls. Dances were held and I did get to one or two - chaperoned by Brenda. I wasn't supposed to be there - in fact our very strict Senior mistress thought we should wear school uniform at all times. We petitioned the Headmaster on one of his visits and he let us wear our own clothes out of school. The Deputy Head was in charge at Thirsk and he postponed his retirement to help out. He died very soon after he did retire.

The people of the town were quite pleasant to us. After all we were flea-free and clean and well-behaved. We didn't cause any trouble at all.

At one stage we gave a concert for them in the school hall. I sang a solo in the Bach Peasant cantata. We also did some P.E. but I can't recall what else.

Sometimes Brenda's house was a bit elastic with visitors. Her niece, about my age, came from Middleham for a few days. The St. Leger, I think, was held at Thirsk that year instead of Doncaster. She took us round the stable area where we met stable boys and horses. The race course was occasionally used by us for sport.

As we were as far as possible away from school I got my mother, a widow, to buy me a bicycle. A lot of us had bikes and we could have runs to Rievaulx, Ripon and Northallerton etc. When I was deep in Higher Exams I let my sister use it and she slightly buckled the front wheel.

Although we were circled with airfields (Brenda's husband was a surveyor who helped to build some), there was never much bombing. Rumours were rife. I remember 'a land mine landed at Crayke' for instance. We once went up Topcliffe Road picking up shrapnel and a house was once bombed in St. James' Green and someone was killed but we had gone home for a few days. Waves of bombers used to go out at dusk and we got quite good at aircraft recognition.

Small things come to my mind. The Station bus, and the little buses bringing people in on Market Day, or taking them out to village 'hops'. Having a tooth out by a travelling school dentist - the most painless extraction I have ever had. The Ritz cinema - still there I believe. Taking a short cut to Stockton Road over the Cod Beck (when it wasn't flooded), Breggins Shop, The Primrose Café and a 'chippy' on the street leading to St. James' Green.

On the whole they were quite happy days although we got a bit homesick now and again. My mother's sister lived at Darlington so we popped over there now and again. Once got stuck in the snow and did not arrive until 2.30 a.m.

The people at Thirsk were very good but you had to be very careful what you said. So many people were related to each other in those days. I don't think it will be the same now somehow.

I left in the following July, after sitting my School Certificate, and went off to King's College - now Newcastle University, where I lived at home. I'd had enough of billets and in those days accommodation at the College was very limited.

Rita Hodgson.

Just a few of the memories I have of my teenage years during the war.

Evacuees arrived in Topcliffe and Asenby from the Durham area. Our village school was very overcrowded, the platform was used as one class and some four classes were taken at different times to accommodate all the pupils.

Long friendships were formed and I still have long phone conversations with my friend who is still interested in Topcliffe and Asenby news. We are both 76 now so we have been friends for 65 years.

Some of the air force wives came to lodge in the village if their husbands were stationed at one of the local aerodromes, and took an active part in our village life.

Classes were held at the Vicarage to cut and roll bandages. Wool was given out for us to knit gloves, scarves and Balaclava helmets. Children gathered hips from the hedgerows, these being made into Rose Hip Syrup.

Members of the Home Guard took turns to keep watch on the top of the church tower to signal any enemy aircraft in the area. We spent many nights as children sleeping under the kitchen table when the sirens sounded.

Many of the forces came to our village Chapel for the Sunday night service, after which we stayed behind and sang favourite hymns round a big coke stove. The ladies of the choir and friends provided tea and cakes which everyone enjoyed. The meeting closed in time for them all to catch a bus back to camp.

The Black Bull Inn was a favourite venue for ham and egg teas, en route to their billets after a long day's flying etc. They were billeted at a girls school just outside Topcliffe which had been taken over for their use.

A very special lady in the village was an old lady called Liza, the local newsagent who delivered the daily papers in an old pram. On returning home she spent the rest of her day washing numerous sets of laundry dropped in by the lads from the camp. The small cottage was always full of steam from shirts, etc. hung up on hangers to dry over a big coal fire. She had no electric washer or drier or even an electric iron. A grand old lady doing her bit for the war.

The village shop got a small supply of cakes in, once in a while. News soon got round and stock soon ran out. Some were kept under the counter for regular customers.

The village fish shop often ran out of fish so we had to resort to meat cakes made with sausage meat inside slices of potato and then fried in batter. They were very tasty and cost 2d each.

At Christmas time dried fruit rations were very small. One old lady got some prunes, dates, figs, etc. and cut them all up into small pieces. She then poured some cream into a screw topped jar and shook it up and down until it turned into butter. Yes, she made her Christmas cake. Almond paste consisted of ground rice and semolina flavoured with almond essence. Tasted quite good!

Tinned fruit was nearly non existent so many housewives spent lots of time bottling fruit as it came to ripen. Shelves were filled with pears, plums, apples, gooseberries, blackcurrants, etc., which were very useful for pies and puddings in winter. Lots of jams and preserves were made. Nothing was wasted.

27ᵗʰ July 1942 (T.R.D.C.)

Letter from the Ministry of Food Catering Officer, stating that the Women's Voluntary Service had made representations to him that there was a necessity for a Pie Scheme in this area as set out in their Circular in relation hereto.

Resolved that the Clerk write to the Ministry of Food Catering Officer asking what branch of the Women's Voluntary Service suggested such a scheme, and also pointing out that the Council was of the opinion that such a scheme was not only unnecessary in this area but also practically unworkable.

The Chairman made reference to the Lord Mayor of London's Air Raid Distress Fund, and said that he wished to thank Mrs. Davies and the Collectors for their efforts during the recent Flag day, and also the members of the Council for their support.

3ʳᵈ August 1942 (diary)

Yesterday a small number of enemy aircraft made tip and run raids on the north-east coast. Damage and casualties were caused but one of the raiders was destroyed.

7ᵗʰ August 1942

AMERICA LANDS 16,000 TROOPS ON THE ISLANDS OF GUADALCANAL IN THE SOLOMON ISLANDS

17ᵗʰ August 1942 (E.A.M.)

Halifax, Mark 5 : crash site near Thirsk 21.10 hours, 1 mile south of Thirsk on the north side of A168 (near Willow Grange) on approach to land at Dalton (relief landing ground). 1 killed and 4 injured.

18ᵗʰ August 1942 (E.A.M.)

Halifax, Mark 2 : near Sowerby. Spun into ground from 1,000' into Green Lane, Sowerby, 18.25 hours whilst returning from an air firing exercise. Pilot and 6 crew killed.

22ᵗʰ August 1942 (D/S)

A White Elephant Stall will be held on Monday, December 7ᵗʰ in Thirsk Market Place. The proceeds will go towards the total of the Thirsk and Wath areas contribution to the Y.W.C.A.'s Special Wartime Appeal. Any contributions for the stall left at Thirsk Hall, by Wednesday, December 2ⁿᵈ will be gratefully received.

2ⁿᵈ September 1942

BATTLE FOR STALINGRAD BEGAN

This battle was to last five months with horrendous casualties on the Russian and German sides.

19th OCTOBER 1942 (T.R.D.C.)

Letter from the Ministry of Health stating that they have issued formal approval of the provision and use for purpose of burials, approximately two acres of land adjoining the existing cemetery at Thirsk.

23rd OCTOBER 1942
BATTLE OF EL ALAMEIN BEGAN

During this five day battle in North Africa, 28,000 Germans and Italians taken prisoner.

15th NOVEMBER 1942
VICTORY IN EGYPT

16th NOVEMBER 1942 (diary)

Yesterday the church bells rang throughout the country to celebrate our victory in Egypt.

18th DECEMBER 1942 (diary)

Last night a number of flares and small bombs were dropped round Topcliffe. Some haystacks were set on fire.

28th DECEMBER 1942 (T.R.D.C.)

Letter from the Hon Secretary of the Canadian Forces Hospitality and Information Service Bureau requesting information as to the organisations which may be willing to help or receive men serving in the Canadian Forces who are in this country.

Resolved that the Clerk furnish the necessary information.

The film that made the most impact on the population during 1942 was 'Mrs. Miniver' starring

---

RADIO PROGRAMMES FOR YULETIDE

KING'S CHRISTMAS DAY BROADCAST

CHRISTMAS DAY

7.0 a.m.—Carol, Time, News.
7.15 app.—Student Songs (records).
7.30—Christmas Day in the Morning.
7.50—Tune In To-day.
8.0—Bernard Crook Quintet.
8.25—Christmas Greetings.
8.45—Christmas Post, 1942. An outside broadcast in which Postman Grubb carries the letters, and Wynford Vaughan Thomas the microphone.
9.0—Carol, Time, News.
9.15 app.—The Kitchen Front.
9.20—The Acceleration Waltz, by Johann Strauss, played by the Minneapolis Symphony Orchestra (records).
9.30—Christmas Day Troops' Service, from St. George's Chapel, Church of the Holy Nativity, Bethlehem. Address by the Rev. F. L. Hughes, M.C., Assistant Chaplain-General, Eighth Army.
10.15—English Songs, sung by Percy Heming (baritone).
10.30—Band of the Manchester Regiment.
11.0—Charles Ernesco, and his Sextet.
11.30—Music by Tchaikovsky (records).
12.10—The Channel Islands. Programme with music.
12.30—Break For Music.
1.0—Time, News.
1.15—B.B.C. Military Band, conductor, P. S. G. O'Donnell.
2.0—The Fourth Christmas. The peoples of the British Commonwealth and their Allies are linked again by radio to greet the men and women everywhere. Incidental music by Victor Hely-Hutchinson. Part 1, The Home Front. Part 2, The Corner-stones. Part 3, The Empire Speaks. Part 4, Christmas with the Forces in Egypt.
3.0—HIS MAJESTY THE KING.
3.40—Pepi, the Polar Bear. Christmas fable for young and old, by Loftus Wigram. Choir, Revue Chorus, B.B.C. Revue Orchestra, and the Dance Orchestra.
4.30—Children Calling Home. British children calling home, with American and Canadian children calling fathers serving with the U.S. and Canadian Forces in this country.
5.0—Carol, Nadolig. Christmas programme in Welsh.
5.20—Children's Hour: The Golden Sail: Scottish Christmas play about Saint Brice, by Robin Stark.
6.0—Time, News.
6.30—News in Norwegian.
6.45—Christmas Party at the Freedom Club. Many who have escaped from occupied Europe are holding their first Christmas Day party in this country.
7.30—Liszt and Chopin, played by Louis Kentner.
8.0—Tommy Handley in Itma, B.B.C. Variety Orchestra, conducted by Charles Shadwell.
8.35—Carols of the Allies: B.B.C. Chorus, conducted by Sir Adrian Boult.
8.54—Wireless For The Blind.
9.0—Time, News.
9.20—Christmas Cackle. Visit the Barnyard. Script by Robert Kemp.
9.45—Sir Isaac Newton.
10.0—B.B.C. Orchestra, conductor Sir Adrian Boult.
10.30—The Plot to Overthrow Christmas. Seasonable extravaganza for broadcasting by Norman Corwin. Produced by Peter Creswell.
11.0—Epilogue.
11.10—Henry Hall and his Orchestra.
12.0—Time, News.

FOR THE FORCES.

6.30 a.m.—Reveille.
7.0—Carol, Time, News.
7.15—Student Songs (records).
7.30—A Musical Christmas Card.
8.0—Christmas Music from Scotland.
8.30—Greetings From Cairo.
9.0—Time, News.
9.15—Christmas Message from Mr. Curtin, Prime Minister of Australia.
9.17—Sidney Torch at the theatre organ.
9.30—York Bowen (piano).
9.45—John Blore and his Orchestra.
10.15—For Isolated Units. Sunday Service, from Rugby Parish Church, conducted by the Rev. H. W. Barnes, Rector of Rugby.
10.30—Band of the Manchester Regiment; conductor, Mr. F. L. Statham.
11.0—Charles Ernesco and his Sextet.
11.30—Carroll Gibbons and his Band.
12.15—Christmas Dinner on a Minesweeper.

Day with Edward Cooper, Cherry Lind, Arthur Marshall, Graham Payn and Athene Seyler, Clive Richardson and Tony Lowry at two pianos.
11.10—Reading from Tennyson's In Memoriam, by Felix Aylmer.
11.20—Henry Hall and his Orchestra.
12.0-12.20—Time, News.

FOR THE FORCES.

6.30 a.m.—Reveille.
7.0—Time, News.
7.15—Band of H.M. Grenadier Guards (records).
7.30—Morning Review.
8.0—Time, News.
8.15—Show Souvenirs (records).
9.0—B.B.C. Military Band.
9.30—H. Robinson Cleaver at the organ of the Granada, Tooting.
9.50—Michaeloff and his Mazurka Orchestra.
10.10—Accent on Rhythm.
10.30—Harry Davidson and his Orchestra.
11.0—Dvorak, Symphony No. 5 in E minor, played by the B.B.C. Scottish Orchestra.
11.45—The Morning After. Christmas gramophone.
12.15—Violin Solos played by Olive Zorian.
1.0—Special Boxing Day Concert.
1.0—Time, News.
1.15—Royal Navy Blue Mariners Dance Septet.
1.45—Mr. Chickery.
2.0—Bickershaw Colliery Band.
2.40—The Captain's Table. Play for broadcasting by Dale Collins.
3.0—Reg. Pursglove and his Orchestra.
3.30—South Sea Island Magic: Record programmes of Hawaiian guitar music.
3.45—Association Football, Army v R.A.F. Commentary during the second half of the match. From Elland Road Ground, Leeds.
4.30—Harry Roy and his Band.
5.0—Welsh Rarebit. They can't stop us singing. Beatrice Botterill (harp), Bobbie Stainforth (piano), the Lyrian Singers.
5.30—Shipmates Ashore. The B.B.C. gives the Merchant Navy a Christmas party at the Merchant Navy Club.
6.0—Time, News, Announcements.
6.30—Sandy's Half-Hour.
7.0—American Sports Bulletin.
7.9—The Yankee Follies of 1942. Concert party, from somewhere in the North.
9.0—Time, News.
9.20—Into Battle. Dramatic presentation of the free peoples of the world at war.
9.30—Billy Ternent and the Dance Orchestra.
10.30—Troise and his Banjoliers.

SUNDAY

7.0 a.m.—Time, News.
7.15—Norman Brooks Berkeley Sextet.
7.45—Carlton Main Frickley Colliery Band, conductor, Albert E. Badrick.
8.15—G. Thalben-Ball plays well-known music for organ.
8.45—The Gospel Singer.
9.0—Time, News.
9.30—Morning Service from St. George's Parish Church, Edinburgh. Address by the Rt. Rev. C. W. G. Taylor, D.D.
10.15—Music For Two Pianos, played by Vitya Vronsky and Victor Babin (records).
10.30—Coventry Hippodrome Orchestra.
11.0—Music-Lover's Calendar.
11.20—Religious Service in Welsh.
11.50—Sandy Macpherson at the theatre organ.
12.10—B.B.C. Scottish Orchestra.
12.50—Mostly For Women.
1.0—Time, News.
1.30—Country Magazine.
1.45—For Home Guards Only.
1.55—Beethoven, played by Denis Matthews.
2.15—In Your Garden.
2.30—Handel's Messiah (Part 1), Isobel Baillie (soprano), Nancy Evans (contralto), Dino Borgioli (tenor), Norman Walker (bass), Liverpool Philharmonic Choir (chorus-master, John Tobin), Liverpool Philharmonic Orchestra (leader, Henry Holst); conductor, Dr. Malcolm Sargent, from the Philharmonic Hall, Liverpool.
4.10—News in Welsh.

Greer Garson and Walter Pidgeon. The vicar in the film was played by Henry Wilcoxon and it is worth quoting his final sermon from the bombed village church. 'This is not only a war of soldiers. It is a war of the people - all of the people - and it must be fought not only in the battlefield but in the cities and villages, in the factories and on the farms, in the homes and in the heart of every man, woman and child who loves freedom.

Well, we have buried our dead, but we shall not forget them. Instead, they will inspire us with an unbreakable determination to free ourselves and those who come after us from the tyranny and terror that threaten to strike us down. This is the people's war.

It is our war. We are the fighters. Fight it, then. Fight it with all that is in us. And may God defend the right.'

CHAPTER SEVEN
1943 - 1944

Bessie Hart, (nee Bradley).

Bessie, who worked in her mother's Mowbray Café in Kirkgate, Thirsk, recalls that the declaration of war in September, 1939, witnessed an influx of service personnel into the town. The race course became a hutted and tented encampment where the King's Own Yorkshire Light Infantry and later the Green Howards would set up their base. A large hut was erected at Castle Garth for the Y.M.C.A. and here dances and concerts were held.

Bessie worked as a volunteer at the Y.M.C.A. and remembers Mrs. Bell, the squire's wife, bringing her pet lamb, bedecked with ribbons, with her. Church House in Kirkgate also continued to provide a venue for concerts and socials. Joan, Bessie's younger sister, was a firm favourite at such gatherings for she had a fine soprano voice. The troops used to love her to sing 'The Holy City'. Every Monday night during the early part of the war Church House provided the venue for a knitting circle. Here gloves, scarves, balaclavas and socks would be knitted and sent to the troops. It was also a good venue for the latest gossip.

Bessie Bradley and Carl Hart

Sunday mornings saw the troops marching from the race course to St. Mary's Church - a fine sight. After the service they were marched to the Market Place where they were dismissed. The vicar's wife, Mrs. Austin, held First Aid classes, for those interested, at the vicarage. At such classes bandages and tourniquets would be applied to fellow students causing a great deal of laughter.

Bessie began courting an officer, Carl Hart, also known as Freddy. Occasionally the manager of the Golden Fleece would arrange dances for officers and their wives or girl friends. These were much more formal occasions than those held at Thirsk Town Hall. The waltz, quickstep, foxtrot and the Palais Glide were some of the dances enjoyed. Bessie's courtship was to last almost the duration of the war for Freddy was in the Sixth Airborne Division which was heavily committed in the war.

Bessie's memories of wartime Thirsk encompass laughter, friendships, helping others and caring. Bessie was asked by a batman to one of the other officers to darn some socks for his officer. The batman brought one over but it really needed a patch rather than a darn. Anyhow she did her best and the officer must have been satisfied with her work as she was brought fourteen pairs of socks. When she had finished Bessie sent a message to say that the darner should at least have a box of chocolates. None ever came.

Bessie's mother used to open the café on a Sunday afternoon so the soldiers could come in and have a chat round the fire (no goods were sold). Here the soldiers would chat, play cards and listen to the wireless. Toast and dripping would make its appearance. On one such occasion, a twenty first birthday was being celebrated when the young soldier burst into song with the words, 'My eyes are dim I cannot see, I have not brought my specs with me!' Bessie believes he was a little tipsy but it certainly enlivened the occasion.

Bessie and Freddy were married by special licence at eight thirty in the morning on the 29th May, 1945 at St. Mary's Church.

11th JANUARY 1943 (T.R.D.C.)

Milk Production complaints have been received from the War Agricultural Executive Committee regarding twelve milk producers in the area for failing to reach market standard for clean milk.

Four premises have been visited, notice served where necessary, and the reports submitted to the War Agricultural Executive Committee. I have again found several churns in dirty condition.

8th FEBRUARY 1943 (T.R.D.C)

Thirsk and Sowerby Salvage. During the month Mr. Wilkinson has held two meetings with the Women's Voluntary Service and other ladies in the forming of a comprehensive scheme for the collection of salvage in Thirsk and

Sowerby and has now arranged a scheme to cover every street, which should lead to a much increased yield of salvage.

Letter from the Ministry of Works and Planning in regard to the proposed Prisoner of War Camp at Thirkleby, and asking if it is possible to provide water for approximately 655 persons.

Joyce Appleton, *(nee Smith)*.

Joyce's early years were spent in the village of Grosmont in the North York Moors. Work was not easy to find in the village and her father found new employment in Thirsk. Settling into a cottage down Mowbray Place and enrolling at Sowerby School Joyce soon made new friends. Hardly had she started school than she became ill. Eventually Dr. Wyon was called and he diagnosed diphtheria. Joyce remembers Dr. Wyon telling her mother off for locking the cottage door, saying, 'There was no need to lock the door.' The doctor arranged for Joyce to be taken by ambulance to the Isolation Hospital at Northallerton and the cottage was disinfected. Visitors to the Isolation Hospital were only allowed on Wednesday and Saturday afternoon and then only to wave to the patients through the glass. Joyce's mother never visited her as she had no means of getting to the hospital while her father used to cycle over when he could. Visiting was eventually curtailed for both parents and patients found it did more harm than good.

To aid her recuperation Joyce returned to Grosmont to stay with an aunt. In 1940 Joyce returned to Thirsk. By now she was eligible to attend the Church School in Piper Lane under the eye of Mr. Mather. Like all the other children she carried her gas mask which was now housed in a new case made by her mother. At home when the siren went the family used to sit on the cellar steps until the All Clear went. She remembers the bombing of Thirsk when Mrs. Crisp was killed on the Green.

Joyce's mother was a good 'contriver'. This meant that she could rustle up a good meal from next to nothing, as well as being good with a needle and thread. As part of the war-time fund raising Joyce's mother organised Whist Drives in the cottage and any money raised would go to the Red Cross Parcels for the troops. Her mother was also a Salvage Steward and encouraged all she met to save paper, jars, bottles, scrap iron etc. for the war effort. Joyce was encouraged to knit and sew and she enjoyed walking and cycling with her friends. On some Sundays she would be allowed to go to the Y.M.C.A. at Castle Garth where she would be treated to a cup of tea, half a sardine sandwich and a finger of cake. The Squire's wife, Mrs Bell, used to play the piano. Mrs. Bell was also noted for bringing a pig or a lamb, on a lead, to the Y.M.C.A.

Canon Broughton of St. Mary's Church initiated an 'At Home Week'. Some form of entertainment was laid on every day of the week and ended with a Rabbit Pie Supper.

Joyce remembers the sterling work that Thirsk Amateurs performed with their many different plays at the Town Hall. Her abiding memories of the war years in Thirsk are of friendly folk united in a common cause.

Don Fothergill.

'In 1939, as a boy of nine years, I lived at Poplar Hill Farm, Asenby, which was in a five mile radius of the aerodromes of Dishforth, Topcliffe, Dalton and Skipton-on-Swale. Dishforth was already operational when the war began, the rest opened early in the 1940s.

The first large aeroplane I saw was a Whitley twin-engine bomber which was the same type I saw crash land at Leckby Palace Farm between Asenby and Cundall. There were no casualties on this occasion.

This area saw at least four more crashes, these being Halifax bombers. I remember one burying itself in the ground and exploding with complete loss of crew. This was my first experience of seeing the devastation first hand. I actually saw parts of limbs strewn over the area as I, and others from local farms, were there before the R.A.F. arrived. I suppose that a boy of my age shouldn't have been there and I was certainly in trouble when I got home.

Some time later, in 1944 or 1945, the R.A.F. were practising towing gliders from Dishforth and one disintegrated over our farm spreading pieces of yellow plywood over the fields and during harvest time I was given the job of picking these pieces up before they got caught in the machinery.

I remember sitting, on summer nights, on a high point in the quarry, which was near our farm, waving to the crews of the Halifax bombers taking off from Dalton. They would always wave back.

Our local roads were always busy through the war years with lorries taking materials from the quarry, R.A.F. lorries, (with bombs and ammunition from Brafferton which were stored in camouflaged Nissen huts) to the local airfields and the Royal Engineers from Ripon camp going to the quarry to fill sand bags.

At one time I saw a German plane flying very low. It machine gunned a farm worker and a horse somewhere near Helperby, killing both.

The Land Army Girls from a hostel near Dishforth aerodrome and the Italian and German P.O.Ws from Thirkleby camp used to come and work on the local farms. I remember the local billeting officer coming to our farm with three sisters aged 6, 9, and 12 (evacuees from Sunderland). They didn't stay long mainly because of the two mile walk to school and back. They didn't take happily to that!

We were all issued with gas masks and at the same time my father had to join the local A.F.S. and was given waterproofs, wellingtons, a stirrup pump and a bucket. If the farm was bombed he would be able to put the fire out with the stirrup pump and bucket!

The pump came in useful as we were able to use it for pumping water out of the cellar where the hams and bacon were stored. We were allowed to kill two pigs a year for the extra staff which were needed on threshing days, harvest, etc. This cellar was used as our air raid shelter.

At the start of the war we had a local lad, Ronnie Appleton, living in. He was called up for army service and came home just once on leave. We never saw him again, he was killed in action, possibly at Dunkirk.

The Canadians used to come to the local village pubs when they were off duty. We used to stand outside and listen to their sing-songs of the war years such as 'Home on the Range, White Cliffs of Dover, A Wing and a Prayer, Me and My Gal, Black Hills of Dakota, and, of course, 'Lilli Marlene'.

I now look back and realise why they enjoyed those nights so much. They never knew who would still be alive, if or when they returned from their bombing raids.

Thinking back and realising how many Canadians were in our area, they must have been a great help.

When the war ended I and other local lads used to stand on Topcliffe Bridge and watch lorries coming through the village taking food and supplies to Dishforth for the Berlin Air lift.'

Ken Wright.

Ken was born in the hamlet of Oldstead seven years before the outbreak of war. The family moved to Thirkleby and it was in this village that Ken's memories of the war are recounted.

Initially he attended Thirkleby School but due to a drop in the number of pupils, it was decided to send the children to Sessay School. Here Miss Rose was head and she had the reputation of being firm but kind. She also had a reputation of being able to 'knock next week's dust out of your jacket.' Ken and the other Thirkleby pupils were generally taken to school in Smith's taxi - a large Armstrong Siddeley car. Monday was an exception for then the Smith's market bus collected the children. This meant a longer journey.

Ken's dad was a noted pig killer for the surrounding area. Folk were allowed to keep pigs but only by following strict Government regulations. He also castrated animals and swept chimneys but his main expertise was the killing of pigs. In this he was assisted by Bill Armstrong, the blacksmith. Ken's dad slaughtered many an illegal pig and received due warning that he and the blacksmith were to be investigated and charged. Bill had numerous sides of bacon hanging up in his cottage and the young Ken Wright was told to take a horse and cart down to Carlton Common. Here he was to unload the cart in the old stone barn and hang the sides of bacon up. He remembers the journey as a real adventure for it was early morning when he set off and he had to have two bicycle lamps strapped to the front of the cart and two on the back. The police, who were some of the main customers of this illegal trade, and the Ministry duly prosecuted and the pair were fined

---

but allowed to keep their instruments of death. The blacksmith had agreed to pay the fine.

One day in March 1943 Ken's dad was stopped going to cultivate a field for Mr. Gibson, the farmer. The Government had requisitioned not only this field but others. The army arrived with wagons and as the vehicles were too large to enter the fields tents and equipment were flung over the hedge. This was the beginning of the Thirkleby Prisoner-of-War Camp. Equipment arrived to push a road in and the area was fenced off with coiled barbed wire. Huts were built and even a football pitch laid out.

The first prisoners to arrive were Italians. They were set to work extending the camp and working on the farms. In their brown uniforms with a yellow diamond on their jackets and trousers they became a familiar sight in this area of Yorkshire. The Italians were followed by German prisoners and finally by Austrians. Colonel Crater was the first Officer Commanding and he quickly acquired an Italian batman who used to collect eggs, butter and bacon from the farm. These were always paid for by the Colonel. There were many skilled craftsmen among the prisoners and joiners were in high demand round the neighbouring farms. Ken recalls the prisoners making slippers with twine, cigarette cases from scrap metal and many other items. Initially the prisoners were taken by wagon round the farms under guard. Later this was relaxed and many allowed to cycle unescorted.

Thirkleby Prisoner-of-War Camp became a focal point for village social life. Here once a week E.N.S.A. would put on a performance. Weekly dances were arranged and people came from the surrounding villages. There was also a weekly Whist Drive and an opportunity to play table tennis and dominoes. A number of prisoners were absorbed into the local community after the war.

8th March 1943 (T.R.D.C.)

Circular No.2766 notifying the Council that arrangements had been made for this Council to erect 8 houses under the Wartime Emergency Programme for housing of Agricultural Workers.

3rd April 1943 (E.A.M.)

Wellington, Mark 3. Due to unauthorised low flying, aircraft hit an electricity pylon on Manor Farm, South

NATIONAL SALVAGE CAMPAIGN
This is to Certify that
MRS C. SMITH.
has been appointed a
SALVAGE STEWARD
By the Thirsk Rural District Council *Council*
Signed Robt. Walker *Date* 8.3.43
s.P.36
WASTE INTO WEAPONS

Kilvington, and crashed while on an air test flight at 15.30 hours. Pilot and 6 crew injured (three of whom were ground staff who went along for the ride).

25th APRIL 1943 (diary).

No important changes in the world's war fronts. From today the church bells are to ring again.

5th MAY 1943 (E.A.M.)

Halifax, Mark 2 : crashed near Sutton Bank. Flew into hillside at Hood Grange Farm at 4.43 hours on route to Leeming whilst being diverted there due to fog after returning from operations. Pilot and two crew seriously injured, five killed.

8th MAY 1943

WINGS FOR VICTORY WEEK

9th MAY 1943

GERMAN FORCES SURRENDER IN TUNISIA

Some 250,000 Italian and German soldiers taken prisoner.

Wings for Victory at Topcliffe. Target £3,500. The opening by Wing-Commander C.C. Sparling (2nd left) Rev C. H. Pauling, Vicar (left), Mr Burton, Schoolmaster (right). Target passed Saturday 8th May, altogether we saved £5,562

16th MAY 1943

DAM BUSTERS RAID

A raid by eighteen bombers on the Mohne, Eder and Sorpe dams. These dams controlled the water for the industrial Ruhr. Of the 113 bomber crew who took part, 56 were killed. The raid was counted a success and is also remembered for Barnes Wallis's 'bouncing bomb'.

Bombing raids continued throughout 1943 on German towns and cities as well as bombing raids on Japanese targets.

14th JUNE 1943. (T.R.D.C.)

Contract for Rats Destruction.

I ask for authority for the War Agricultural Executive Committee to undertake the clearance of rats at our Salvage Depot, Thirsk Junction, at a cost of £3 per year.

28th JUNE 1943 (T.R.D.C.)

Letter from the Ministry of Health stating that the following consultation with the Ministry of Labour and National Service, certain categories of married women with household responsibilities should be encouraged to take in land workers in lieu of ordinary industrial employment.

Kay Konieczny, (nee Hall).

Kay's mother ran a café in Finkle Street for many years. Growing up in Thirsk during the war meant adapting to changing fortunes. One of Kay's earlier memories is of the number of poster competitions that were aimed at children. Such posters were to encourage the civilian population to further efforts, whether saving money, fuel or food. The barometer in the Market Place kept track of the amount raised for various events and great was the excitement when the projected target was reached, then exceeded.

The Home Guard often used the alleyways and back-yards of the Finkle Street shops and houses when on manoeuvres. The Home Guard members, forage caps pulled well down would hide then pounce on their 'enemies' as they moved from building to building. Great excitement to a young child. The wireless was a great favourite with Kay. 'Children's Hour' with Uncle Mac bidding, 'Good night children everywhere.' still haunts her. She also enjoyed 'The Ovaltineys', I.T.M.A., and the 'Crazy Gang'. The Regent and the Ritz cinemas offered other types of entertainment. Mr. Ward was the manager of the Regent Cinema while Mr. Buck managed the Ritz. Mr. Buck was noted for his loud voice, which he often used to quell unruly youngsters. At these cinemas Kay would watch the singing and dancing of Shirley Temple, The Three Stooges, Tarzan, Mrs. Miniver as well as the all important Pathe News.

The Dole Office was in Finkle Street. This later, possibly 1943, was taken over by the Air Force and it became the Canadian Post Office which became especially busy in the run up to Christmas.

In 1939 the Royal Engineers from Sunderland set up camp at Stoneybrough. The first winter was a test of endurance as it was a severe winter and the soldiers were under canvas. By June 1940 the camp was complete with large Nissen huts, brick and timber huts, roads, showers and the stores - very important. Thirsk quickly became a military town but the civilian population was not neglected. Dances in the Town Hall and Sowerby Parochial Hall attracted professional big bands. Concerts were also held with touring E.N.S.A. groups who performed plays and other light entertainment. The civilians embraced such entertainment with gusto.

Military and air force personnel and the women's services swelled the local population. The Women's Land Army and The Timber Corps were not unfamiliar to the people of Thirsk. Due to petrol rationing a number of farmers resorted to coming to market with horses and carts, ponies and traps. The farmers' wives, Kay remembers, had huge baskets of fruit and eggs together with a range of other locally produced goods for sale. Many people grew their own vegetables especially following a 'Dig for Victory' campaign. Victory in Europe, (V.E. Day), saw a number of street parties around the Green and Market Place. Red, white and blue were the colours of the day as sing-a-longs rivalled one another. Victory over Japan, (V.J. Day), followed some weeks later though the celebrations were not so boisterous. The years from 1939 to 1945 were never easy but the community was united in a common cause - victory.

Blackout Times

NORTH RIDING

	Begins. p.m.	Ends. a.m.
Today (Sat.)	11.23	4.46
Sunday	11.24	4.46
Monday	11.25	4.45
Tuesday	11.25	4.45
Wednesday	11.26	4.45
Thursday	11.26	4.45
Friday	11 27	4.45
Saturday	11.27	4.45

COUNTY DURHAM

	Begins. p.m.	Ends. a.m.
Today (Sat.)	11.41	4.30
Sunday	11.42	4.30
Monday	11.43	4.29
Tuesday	11.43	4.29
Wednesday	11.44	4.29
Thursday	11.44	4.29
Friday	11.45	4.29
Saturday	11 45	4.29

30th June 1943
DOMINATION OF THE SOLOMON SEAS
In the Far East General MacArthur began the conquest of those islands in the Solomon Seas the Japanese had previously conquered.

Mrs. Myra Otterburn, *(nee Bell).*
Leaving school at fourteen years of age Myra began her working life as a counter assistant at a confectioners in Castle Gate in Thirsk. Later she moved to Moss's Grocers Shop in the town, for more money. This was a busier establishment and the hours were from 8a.m. until 6p.m., including Saturdays. Myra enjoyed serving the customers and the shop was particularly

busy on market days. Once a week there was a 'weighing up' day when some of the staff would weigh up the sugar into blue bags and other commodities into different coloured bags. It was very important not to spill anything and to make sure the tops of the bags were folded properly. Once war had been declared and food rationing began people had to register with one shop. Ration books were marked and coupons cut out as the strictly limited food was purchased. Myra was told to be very careful and strict and to show no favours to anyone.

Her father died in 1942 and she was deferred from conscription because of this. At the beginning of 1943 a brown envelope bearing the initials O.H.M.S. arrived and she was ordered to report to the N.A.A.F.I. at Linton-on-Ouse. Issued with a rather smart khaki uniform she began her training as a manageress of a N.A.A.F.I. canteen.

Myra Otterburn (nee Bell) 30th June 1943

These canteens were set up as and when required, and served cakes, coffee and the all important cup of tea. No cooked meals were served and the canteen opened for a short while in the morning, again at lunch-time and finally from six in the evening.

Posted to Dalton WAAF. Station she continued her role as manageress. Nissen huts provided accommodation and Myra with the cook and two other conscripts made the best of her new posting. The District Manager of the N.A.A.F.I. used to visit to check the accounts and the ordering and sale of food. Everything had to be spick and span for such a visit. Dalton was handy for short visits home and Myra caught either Mr. Smith's little bus, which ran a service from the villages, or cycled. By now her mother was billeting an evacuee, a Maureen Harmon, who came from the Brixton area. Maureen was not only company but a welcome addition to the family budget.

As the war drew to a close Myra transferred to the W.A.R.A.G. and became the assistant warden at the hostel for Land Army girls. She was then posted to Alne Hall, near York, to work until she was finally demobbed in 1945.

9th August 1943 (T.R.D.C.)

Sketch plan 'Home Guard Hut' Topcliffe

A sketch plan has been submitted by Mr. W.T. Sigsworth, Commander of the Home Guard at Topcliffe, for permission to erect a Wood Hut 50ft. by 15ft. to be used as a headquarters for the Home Guard. The hut is to be erected in a walled enclosure at Dean's Square in Topcliffe.

It is proposed to use the conveniences and water supply at the Angel Hotel, Topcliffe. If this proposal is approved it should only be for a limited period. Closet and urinal accommodation should be provided on site, and a condition should be made that the hut is approved only as a Meeting Place and not for sleeping purposes under ordinary circumstances.

Recommended that this be approved subject to the approval of the Town Planning Committee.

17th August 1943

SICILY IN ALLIED HANDS

Following thirty-six days of fighting, the island of Sicily was in Allied hands.

28th August 1943 (D/S)

Funds for local members of H.M. Forces Whist Drive (Sept. 8th, 8 p.m.); Dance (Sept.15th, 8-12 p.m.) Music by Night Birds Band. Please support this good cause.

3rd September 1943

ITALY INVADED

Following the fall from power of Mussolini and the increasing success of the resistance movement in those countries occupied by Germany, Allied troops invaded, under the leadership of General Montgomery, mainland Italy.

4th October 1943 (T.R.D.C.)

Book Drive; books received totalled 40,594 of which 3,753 were allocated to the Forces and 100 to Libraries, Hospitals etc. The total weight of books sent for repulping was 7tons.11cwts.2 qtrs.

15th October 1943 (E.A.M.)

Halifax, Mark 2 : damaged on take off due to wide swing and hitting obstruction. Managed to become airborn but soon lost height and crashed into Farmer Chapman's field, Stockton Road, South Kilvington, 11.25 hours. Three crew injured.

16th OCTOBER 1943 (D/S)

The lively exchange of opinion on the merits and demerits of Topcliffe Royal Charter Fair voiced at a recent meeting of residents has stirred interest over a wide area. Strong arguments adduced in favour of the abolition of the Fair were countered by equally effective contentions in favour of retention. In the end a motion to liquidate the Fair was defeated by a slight majority.

25th OCTOBER 1943

RAILWAY OF DEATH COMPLETED

The Burma-Thailand Railway, known to all who worked on it as the 'Railway of Death', was completed. Some 16,000 prisoners of war who had been forced by the Japanese to work on the railway died from disease, starvation and ill-treatment.

Jean Cave *(nee Jewitt)*

War mongering was part of life prior to 1939. Jean knew little of the drama unfolding in Europe. Even the excitement of being issued with a gas mask did not intrude on her prowess as an athlete. Jean represented her school at running and loved every aspect of sport. Her greatest ambition at that time was to pass her eleven plus to go the Grammar School in Topcliffe Road. To this end she prayed mightily for help from above. The names of those pupils who had been successful were read out by the head teacher at school assembly. Five of Jean's year had their names read out. Among the five was the name of Jean Jewitt. Her father was delighted while her mother had reservations about her success for jobs were not plentiful and it would mean her staying on until she was at least sixteen. As a reward for her success Jean's dad bought her a Royal Enfield Bicycle. This was purchased at Harry Hyde's shop on Topcliffe Road. Such was Jean's pride in owning such a bike that she wheeled it rather than rode it from the shop.

In September 1939 Jean was not a little anxious to don her new uniform and start her new school. Uncertainty was the order of the month for all pupils were told to watch for and read a notice which would be put on the school gates. The notice would inform them when the school would open for the Autumn term. Eventually Jean was able to realise her dream as she stepped over the threshold of the Grammar School.

Other influences were at work in the Jewitt household. The first wave of evacuees with their teachers, had arrived from Gateshead. The Jewitt home was on the official list to house one evacuee. Jean said to her mother, 'be sure to bring back a little girl.' The evacuees were herded, along with their teachers, into Sowerby Parochial Hall. Jean's mother thought it was just like a cattle mart and was horrified at the selection process. Much to Jean's surprise her mother came back with three eleven year old boys; two brothers Teddy and Ronnie and a boy called Edmund. Jean records a number of memories about these lads. First she had new playmates and spent hours in the garden with them trying to tunnel to Australia. The three boys had head lice and did not know how to use a knife and fork and they found it very difficult to adjust to rural life. When the parents of the evacuees visited their offspring many decided to take them home. This was the case with Teddy, Ronnie and Edmund. Jean believes they flourished during the short period of time they were in Thirsk and Sowerby.

The second wave of Evacuees came in 1941/42. Once again they were from Gateshead and this time Jean got her wish. .Gladys Stephenson was a pupil at Gateshead Grammar School and was billeted with the Jewitts. Initially, because of the number of additional pupils, the children went to the Grammar School in the morning and then either to Church House or the school room at the Salem Chapel. This timetable alternated between Thirsk and Gateshead Grammar schools. Miss Watson started a 'Girls Club' in Barnet's yard, Thirsk. This ran during the week from 6 - 8 p.m. and was well supported. Table tennis was played, the girls were taught how to make leather gloves and moccasins by a lady from Bagby while Dr. Addison taught First Aid. Dr. Addison is remembered for waving bones at a not altogether too attentive group of girls.

Thirsk market continued to operate during the war. The farmers and their wives brought their produce in - eggs, butter, poultry and rabbits to sell. They did this on the north side of the Market Place and a lively day was generally enjoyed. The market stall-holders occupied the other side of the Market Place. Here Jean's mother would buy material to make clothes. Outside the Post Office at that time a huge model thermometer was erected. This was coloured week by week as the total amount of National Savings of the town was recorded for all to see. An offshoot of the Savings Scheme was the introduction of a school bank where money could be saved to help the country's war effort.

'Dig for Victory' was encouraged and people were urged by the Government to grow their own vegetables. The garden at Jean's home was put to good use and all hands were put to work growing potatoes, peas, onions, leeks, cabbage, beans, carrots, as well as soft fruit. Jean's mum was a good provider and produced four good meals a day.

All were taken at the table. Breakfast was generally porridge, egg on fried bread or with bacon, while dinner at noon was a meat and vegetable dish followed by a pudding. Jean's favourite was steamed roly-poly. At five in the afternoon tea was taken and usually some sort of savoury such as pork pie, cooked ham or cheese. Supper was a warm up from dinner - cold meat, fried potatoes or sandwiches. Compulsory billeting took many forms during wartime. Three workmen were billeted with the Jewitt family. These men were working on the airfield at Dalton. Jean's dad played cards with them usually nine card brag. The stakes were a halfpenny and very occasionally Jean was allowed to play. On one occasion an air-raid took place and the work which the men had done that day was destroyed. The raid was also remembered as one of the men, Ted, struggled to put on his trousers as he 'wanted to die decent!'

Jean's mother also let rooms to officer's wives and other civilians. One of these was an Indian called Guy Fuller, remembered by Jean because he possessed an incredible fourteen pairs of shoes!! Jean was paid sixpence for cleaning them. Those who stayed helped Jean in other ways. Writing essays was always a hardship and Jean used to persuade the officers' wives to write them for her. Unfortunately the teacher soon realised that such work was not that of Jean.

Jean also remembers Mr. Tillet, the head teacher, saying to Mr. Greenwood, another teacher of Jean, 'you know the pattern on the back of her cardigan better than the front,' as she was noted for turning round and chatting to those behind her.

The SQUANDER BUG
WILL GET YOU IF YOU DON'T WATCH OUT!

When the Squander Bugs put their heads together there's trouble brewing! They're out to stop your money helping the war. They'll do all they can to prevent you having a little nest-egg when peace comes. Fortunately, more and more sensible people are defeating them by buying Savings Certificates regularly every week. Are *you* one of them?

Savings Certificates costing 15/- are worth 20/6 in 10 years— increase free of income tax. They can be bought outright, or by instalments with 6d., 2/6 or 5/- Savings Stamps through your Savings Group or centre, or at any Post Office or Trustee Savings Bank. Buy now!

ISSUED BY THE NATIONAL SAVINGS COMMITTEE

He also told the pupils of the school not to pick up any strange objects that they may find. One boy, who cycled to school, ignored the advice and had two fingers blown off one of his hands as a result. The device was probably a butterfly bomb dropped by the Germans.

Few air-raid shelters were available in the town. Mr. Jewitt became a fire watcher and was given a stirrup pump and a bucket. When the siren went they sheltered under the stairs and played Snap by candlelight.

Leisure activities depended on which age group you were in. Sheep were grazed on the school field and hay-making was also carried out. This gave the youngsters, including Jean, an opportunity to build camps and make a ball out of hay, to play with. Jean also had a pair of roller skates and loved to hang on the back of a bike for an extra long skate. She once got as far as Bagby. Fishing with nets on sticks along the Cod Beck was yet another pastime. Castle Garth was a favourite place for sledging until a tank trap was built there and spoilt it all. The cinema also gave great pleasure. James Mason was her favourite film star in such films as 'The Night Has Eyes.' Margaret Lockwood who starred in 'The Wicked Lady' was another idol. The noise generated by scores of children at the matinees did not appeal to young Jean. The wireless also provided entertainment with such programmes as 'Dick Barton, Special Agent' and the music of the orchestra of the day. There were lots of competitions for posters with good slogans. Jean won a huge box of paints at the beginning of the war in a competition organised by Timothy Whites. She also won a free ticket for the cinema for colouring a poster of Sabu.

Jean's older sister, Betty, had married and moved to Norwich. Jean was sent on holiday there and changed trains three times. First at Peterborough, then at March and finally she changed at Ely. While at Norwich a bombing raid took place and she had her first experience of sheltering under a Morrison shelter. This was a steel topped table with wire mesh along the sides. It also acted as a dining table.

Throughout the 1939/45 war Jean met some excellent people in the small friendly Yorkshire town she grew up in. Her memories are of a caring community who did their best for the transient military and civilian personnel as well as for the war effort.

2ⁿᵈ NOVEMBER 1943
KILLINGS AT MAJDANEK
Some 45,000 survivors of the Warsaw ghetto killed by machine gun fire in one week by German soldiers.

Frank (Tanner) Smith.
Frank was at Church with his parents when war broke out. It seemed a day of emotional despair for the memories of the 1914/18 war were still relatively fresh. Not only were evacuees now living with the Smiths in the Crescent but also officers' wives. Frank's dad became an Air Raid Warden and Frank saw the black-out descend on Thirsk and the surrounding villages. The black-out was a new experience as was the influx of military forces in and around the town which caused its own excitement. Frank watched with some amazement and concern as buildings were requisitioned, gas masks were issued, rationing imposed and hundreds, it seemed, of regulations imposed on the civilian population. By 1940 Frank had had enough and at 18 years of age he volunteered rather than wait to be conscripted. He left Thirsk to join the West Yorks. His memories of pre-war Thirsk still linger. The cottages and fields, the market days on Mondays and Saturdays, the outings to Sutton Bank on Good Friday, the increasing mechanical transport and the smoking chimneys.

Such memories would remind him that after the shouts of the Sergeant Major there was a place called home - Thirsk.

6ᵗʰ NOVEMBER 1943
KIEV RE-TAKEN BY THE RUSSIANS
Kiev was Russia's largest town.

Richard Chapman.

Richard recalls bombs being transported to Topcliffe and Skipton-on-Swale aerodromes from the bomb dumps. Not infrequently they came off their trolleys, especially at Tollbooth Corner in Topcliffe. As a young lad he was scared but the Canadian airmen went and sat on the bombs waiting for help to re-load. The airmen told them not to worry as the bombs were not primed.

One of the advantages of the siren going off after 10 or 11 o'clock at night was that there was no school the following morning, until 10 or 11 the next day. Many families went into the cemetery when the sirens sounded and sheltered under the large fir trees.

The shrapnel collected from bombing raids became much sought after. It was collected from the bomb craters and was a prized possession.

Richard lived at 3, Council Houses, Topcliffe and had a Sergeant Pilot staying with the family. Once the young pilot had his girl friend up from Ipswich to stay with him.

Richard's mother was very upset when she found out they weren't married.

Richard and his dad witnessed a Whitley bomber crash on take off. The bomber failed to gain height and came down. The crew didn't stand a chance. Richard's dad threw him into a gutter and himself on top as the ammunition went off. They were there for twenty minutes.

Fishing took on a new meaning when the soldiers went fishing with hand grenades. The grenades were lobbed into the river and the stunned fish collected for cooking.

There was a welcome home party held in the school main room for all who had served in the forces. Tommy Bentall and his wife served up fish, chips and peas, bread and butter and tea. Some of the locals made speeches.

5 lbs. OF COAL SAVED IN ONE DAY BY 40,000 HOMES WILL PROVIDE ENOUGH FUEL TO BUILD A CHURCHILL TANK

NOTE: 5 lbs. of coal are used in 2 hours by a gas fire or electric oven.

Is YOUR home saving fuel to make Churchill tanks?

Save FUEL for BATTLE

ISSUED BY THE MINISTRY OF FUEL AND POWER.

13th DECEMBER 1943 (T.R.D.C.)

Letter from the Ministry of Health.

Sir,

Housing of the Working Classes.

Post War Programme.

I am directed by the Minister of Health to refer to Circulars 2778 and 2802 and to the programme of 90 houses submitted by your Council. I am to remind you, that, although the selected sites are already in your Council's possession action should be taken by consultation with the Planning Authority and with the Minister of Agriculture and Fisheries (through the County War Agricultural Executive Committee) to make sure they are free from objections on planning and agricultural grounds. I am to ask that you will confirm that this action has been taken, and that there are no objections as far as your Council's programme is concerned.

29th DECEMBER 1943

BERLIN RAIDED

The bombing of German cities continued unabated including raids on the German capital, Berlin. Hitler's tyranny against the Jews, the Russian prisoners of war, and fighters in the resistance movement also continue unabated.

CHAPTER EIGHT
1944 - 1945

8th JANUARY 1944 (D/S)
Dalton, (Thirsk).

A dance will be held on Tuesday, January 18th 1944 in Messrs Higgs and Hills Dining Hall. Dancing from 8p.m. to 12 midnight. Admission 2/-. In aid of Red Cross and St. John's Fund. Night Birds Band.

17th JANUARY 1944 (T.R.D.C.)

Ambulance Register; The Ambulance Register was submitted showing that in the nine months ending 31st December the Ambulance had been called out 137 times, a travelling distance of 5,248 miles and £27.8s had been charged for the use of the Ambulance by non-ratepayers 24th January 1944.

Correspondence:- Councillor F. Lambert raised the question that there is no provision for members of the forces to obtain refreshments when having to wait for considerable amounts of time on Thirsk Railway Station.

Resolved that the rail company be approached with a view to obtaining such facilities.

27th JANUARY 1944
LENINGRAD FREED

The siege of Leningrad was finally resolved after lasting over two and a half years.

5th FEBRUARY 1944 (D/S)
Test of Air Raid Sirens.

Public air raid sirens will be tested at 10a.m. on Monday throughout Northumberland, Durham and the North Riding. The 'raider passed' signal will be sounded for one minute then the 'alert' for one minute only and finally the 'raiders passed' signal again for one minute. The test will not be made in any district in which an actual 'alert' has been sounded during the previous fortnight.

7th FEBRUARY (T.R.D.C.)
Proposed Central Kitchen for Board of Education:-

Plan submitted by the Ministry of Works showing proposed site of Central Kitchen for School Meals.

The building is to be erected adjoining the new Ministry of Food Store Shed, facing Melbourne Place.

Recommended that this be approved.

Briefing for Berlin 424-433 Squadrons - Skipton-on Swale 15th February 1944

12th FEBRUARY 1944 (D/S)
Farm Workers and Their Meals.
Food Ministry's Two Concessions.

Col. Llewellyn, Food Minister, has announced two food concessions for agricultural workers. Their present extra supplies of tea, sugar, margarine, cheese, preserves and milk, where necessary at harvest, hay-time, sheep shearing, lambing and threshing may now be issued by farmers to their workers to be cooked or prepared in their homes.

Hitherto the extra supplies for workers had to be used either by the farmers in preparing meals for the workers, or, if issued to the workers, had to be eaten in the fields, not taken to their homes.

In many farmhouses help had so diminished that it was not possible for the farmers to prepare workers' meals said the Minister, and in consequence the extra supplies had, in some cases, not been taken up by the employers.

The second concession consists of an extra half point per day per worker during these periods. This will enable more variety to be introduced into the meals of farm workers.

Volunteers for farm work during these periods if resident on the farms will share in these allowances.

26th FEBRUARY 1944 (D/S)
Thirsk Young Farmers Club.

Dance will be held in the Parochial Hall, Sowerby on Monday, March 6th 1944. Music by the Night Birds Orchestra. Dancing 8p.m. to midnight. Tickets 2/6.

5th MARCH 1944

GLIDER DROP

In Burma, British, Gurkha and Indian soldiers were flown by glider behind Japanese lines.

20th MARCH 1944 (T.R.D.C)

Correspondence:- Letter from the C.O. of a local unit requesting the Council to give favourable consideration to any application for the opening of cinemas in Thirsk on Sunday evening. As the application did not state whether the person was duly authorised by the Army Council or Air Council to furnish such a certificate for the purposing of this Regulation, no action was taken.

27th MARCH 1944 (T.R.D.C.)

Skipton Bridge Water.

The Clerk submitted a letter from the District Water Company, stating that it was impossible for them to obtain the necessary permission to supply the whole of the village of Skipton Bridge from the Air Ministry water main.

Recommended that the previous scheme of erecting a pillar tap in the village be proceeded with.

Thirkleby Water.

The Clerk submitted a letter from Mr. Dunlop stating that he was receiving a very intermittent supply at his farm and asking that something be done forthwith. The Financial Officer reported on the position in regard to the Camp supply and it was Recommended that the Ministry of Works be communicated with, asking them to make arrangements for all water to be drawn from their Storage tank which will be filled during the hours of 10p.m. and 6a.m. next morning.

> # Do not invade the trains THIS EASTER
>
> It is the duty of us all to help keep the railways free for the movement of men and materials for our Fighting Forces. So — don't travel this Easter.
>
> **RAILWAY EXECUTIVE COMMITTEE**

17ᵗʰ APRIL 1944 (T.R.D.C)

Opening of Sunday Cinemas.

The Clerk submitted a certificate from the Brigadier for the Northern District under the Defence regulation No.42B (1939) stating that he was of the opinion that it was expedient that places licensed under the Cinematograph Act 1909 should be opened on Sunday. Councillor Forster moved and Councillor Earle seconded that the Council take the necessary steps to obtain the order for Sunday Opening of Cinemas under Defence Regulation 42B (1939).

On being put to the meeting there voted for the motion 10, and against the motion 10, whereupon the Chairman gave his casting vote against the motion. The motion was then declared lost.

15ᵗʰ APRIL 1944 (E.A.M.)

Crashed one mile south west of Thirsk after overshooting Dishforth runway because of engine failure and loss of height. Hit a house near railway bridge on B1448 road. One engine fouled railway line and one pair of houses flattened. 5 crew killed, 2 injured.

24ᵗʰ APRIL 1944 (E.A.M.)

Halifax, Mark 3, spun into the ground near Sowerby Parks Farm whilst performing tight turns during a flight affiliation exercise. All nine crew killed.

6ᵗʰ MAY 1944 (D/S)

Thirsk Rural District Water Co. Ltd.

To the inhabitants of Thirsk and Kilvington, particularly Market Place, Thirsk, Millgate, The Green, Stammergate, etc. The water supply to the above will be interrupted from time to time next week for short periods during valve repairs etc.

C.R.Pinkney. Secretary.

8ᵗʰ MAY 1944 (T.R.D.C.)

A.R.P. Mortuary;- Both civilian and R.A.F. bodies were received into the Mortuary on the Sunday morning following the bomber crash on Railway Cottages, Topcliffe Road of Saturday night, 15ᵗʰ April 1944 in which one house was totally destroyed.

6ᵗʰ JUNE 1944

D - DAY

Allied Forces, under the leadership of General Eisenhower, landed on the beaches of Normandy in the greatest invasion known to man.

SALUTE THE SOLDIER WEEK

July 10th - 17th

THIRSK, SOWERBY AND DISTRICT

OBJECTIVE £80,000

Pearl Marshall. *As told by her daughter.*

Pearl was born Pearl Marshall on the 21st May 1924. She was born in Bell Terrace in the West End of Newcastle. She was brought up by her Grandmother and relatives, her Aunt Sarah and Uncle Alf.

Alfred Salton, B.E.M., came from Easingwold, worked on the railway and settled up here in Newcastle after marrying Sarah. When Pearl was five years old they took her for a holiday to a little place called Boltby, near Thirsk, staying at a place called 'Ivy Cottage' (at the time belonging to one of Alf's cousins called Sarah also).

When war broke out Pearl tried to get in the Land Army but she was too young.

The war was still raging a couple of years later and she finally joined up being posted to the Lake District.

After a few months they told her she was being posted to North Yorkshire, near a little place called Boltby, not far from Thirsk. She couldn't believe it. It was more than a coincidence.

She spent many a happy time there. A lot of the girls together from all walks of life, from the roughest part of the East End of London, to one being titled 'the Right Honourable such and such.' They all just mucked in together.

One memory she told me was when they worked with the German prisoners of war on the land. One was called Hans. He came from Graz in Austria and another was called Rudi. He apparently had been the Olympic Ski Champion and wore the jumper with the Olympic rings on, just an unfortunate young man caught in the conflict of war.

One Saturday she would come home to Newcastle - the other week-end she would stay at the camp and go into Thirsk.

Any 'dates' they had were met at the Clock in Thirsk. A couple of the girls had Canadian/American boy friends (pilots I think).

Anytime I'm passing through Thirsk I always think of her when I look at that Clock

She said that one week-end they got drunk on cider and couldn't find their way back to the camp.

Another time they got landed with an American sergeant who was really worse for wear. They asked their head of camp, a rather 'posh' lady (lah dee dah my mam called her) if they could put him up for the night. She said, 'No

---

way, what would the locals think - Americans sleeping at an all ladies camp.' So they finally found the old postmaster. I think they called him Danny Counten and he put him up for the night. Apparently he got a shock when he woke up and saw an old man wandering about in his long johns.

She was attached to the Timber Corps camp and spent many hot summer days working in the woods, felling down the trees.

The camp consisted of 4 Nissen huts and two concrete buildings, showers, toilets and a dining hall. One was a recreation room. Being in the country there was no electric.

Boltby was exactly the same as she remembered it from the holiday in 1929. She says that the villages in North Yorkshire are hard to equal anywhere in the world. When she arrived in Thirsk to join her post she had a cup of tea in a local café and enquired the best way to get to Boltby. Two R.A.F. pilots at the next table replied, 'You will be lucky to get a bus once a week!' She had to get a taxi from two very genteel ladies who ran a taxi service from their home.

As I said, she spent many a happy time in the Land Army/Timber Corps cycling into Thirsk during the week after they finished work. It turned out to be one of the happiest times in her life, so some good came out of war.

She went on to marry a Polish man, my father, and had two daughters, Greta and Karin.

Sadly Pearl died in 1998.

Crash at Skipton-on-Swale 5th August 1944

ON THIS SITE IN AUGUST 1944 A DISABLED ROYAL CANADIAN AIR FORCE HALIFAX III BOMBER CRASHED ON RETURN FROM A BOMBING MISSION, RESULTING IN THE DEATHS OF TWO CREW MEMBERS AND ONE CIVILIAN.

THIS CAIRN, IN THE SHADE OF A CANADIAN MAPLE TREE, IS ERECTED TO HONOUR ALL THOSE WHO SERVED WITH THE RCAF SIX GROUP SQUADRONS AT SKIPTON ON SWALE DURING WWII, AND THE MANY CIVILIANS WHO SUPPORTED THEM. MAY THEIR ENTERPRISE, COURAGE AND DEVOTION TO DUTY BE REMEMBERED AND SERVE AS AN INSPIRATION TO ALL.

DEDICATED MAY 19, 1984 BY A GROUP INCLUDING GRATEFUL SURVIVORS.

'THIS WAS THEIR FINEST HOUR'

The Cairn at Skipton-on-Swale

Rose Stothard. *Resident of Thirsk.*

Rose worked as a waitress at The Golden Fleece Hotel during the war and remembers that a market stall holder sold black stockings at what seemed an exorbitant price. The stockings were always faulty and one pair she bought had seams at the side.

'Such is war!' the stall holder said when she complained.

Maurice Sanderson.

Maurice Sanderson's parents farmed at Skipton-on-Swale some six miles from Thirsk. In 1933 he was enrolled as a pupil at Catton School where the head-teacher was Mrs. Lynch. Another member of staff was a Miss Wilkinson. The school served the villages of Catton, Baldersby, Howe and Skipton-on-Swale.

In 1939 the head-teacher asked the pupils to go to Skipton Methodist Church on Saturday afternoon. They were greeted by Mr. Bainbridge who had brought a tin bath full of gas masks. These had to be fitted by adjusting the straps which held the mask on. The children were told they had to wear them at all times and had to look after them. The threat of a gas attack from the air seemed very real.

In May Mr. Sanderson was informed that the Government was going to requisition some of his land in order to build an airfield. There would be no appeal. A labour force was assembled and set to work. Fences, hedges and trees were uprooted. The brush-wood was burnt and the contractors gave the firewood to the villagers, a welcome gift.

Maurice listened to Prime Minster Chamberlain's address on the wireless with his parents when they learned that they were officially at war. This did not prevent Maurice from entering the Grammar School in Thirsk that September. He cycled to school and recalls the taped up windows, the siren instructions when they all had to go into the corridor with their gas masks.

He also remembers that when they went potato picking Mr. Tillet, the head-master, 'nearly went spare,' as their school work was being neglected.

At home a barrage balloon, which had escaped from its moorings, was shot down by a tail gunner in a Whitley aircraft. The ladies of the village knitted comforts for the troops and the Women's Institute went to work bottling fruit in kilner jars and being lectured on how to make the best use of rations. Certain tradesmen who were after animals for food would leave the farm with the words, 'If it's ill and you're going to shoot it, I'll take it.' Maurice watched in disbelief as signposts were taken down. In place of the signposts in the village were nine soldiers and a corporal billeted in an old farm house. Their role was to direct military traffic to either Catterick or Ripon. Another small unit was billeted in the village and their purpose was to prepare the bridge at Skipton-on-Swale for demolition. A great deal of dynamite was stored in the farm buildings. The Local Defence Volunteers were formed in 1940 and a chicken hut was erected on a hill in the village as their headquarters. A bizarre event also occurred at this time for concrete posts were erected on the airfield, (which was not yet operational) to prevent enemy planes landing. Maurice later found out that at this time the German invasion of England was imminent.

It seemed that Skipton-on-Swale had become a war zone. There were gun emplacements all around the village while many trenches were dug for use by the troops should the village be attacked. The concrete posts on the airfield were removed and work began in earnest on the construction of an aerodrome. The main contractor was Wimpey using labour from Tyneside. Concrete runways were built, wood and plasterboard huts appeared, Nissen huts were put together and the all important control tower was built. Eventually the aerodrome became operational and Maurice found himself spending more and more time with service personnel and his school work began to suffer.

The war years proved to be an exciting time. He spent nearly all his spare time on the airfield talking and listening to the hundreds of new servicemen and women. Although the airfield was bombed this did nothing to deter Maurice from his ritual visits. The station cinema was a great attraction and two films he remembers watching were 'National Velvet', with Mickey Rooney and Elizabeth Taylor and 'The Picture of Dorian Gray', starring George Sanders and Angela Lansbury. Maurice became quite skilled at helping the projectionist. On one occasion a film portraying the dangers of venereal diseases was shown on the orders of the Station Commander. Apparently the station was operating below strength because of the number of personnel who had contracted V.D.

Dances were also held on the aerodrome and transport laid on for girls who wished to attend. Girls from as far away as Harrogate came. E.N.S.A. (Entertainments National Service Association) concerts proved another attraction.

Maurice, at this time, was responsible for blowing the church organ in the village. Dr. Temple who was Archbishop of York at the time came to preach and he was most annoyed to find that only a handful of people turned up to hear his sermon.

No poultry was kept on the farm due to the constant theft of the birds. Rabbits were plentiful and found a ready market. Part of the labour force on the farm were Land Army girls and German and Italian prisoners of war. The Land Army girls had to be withdrawn as the R.A.F. personnel used to distract them from their work.

Plane crashes were frequent. One such crash Maurice vividly recalls. This was on the 4th August 1944, just before tea. Maurice and a friend were chatting by the farm gate watching the planes return from a raid over enemy territory. Both boys commented that one of the planes looked very dodgy as it came in to land. A warning rocket fired from the aerodrome suddenly appeared in the sky. This was to indicate to the Halifax that it was not to land but fly a second circuit and then land. Unfortunately a lack of fuel caused the aircraft to lose power before crashing on to the village green. Fortunately the boys had hurled themselves behind a wall and so escaped the exploding plane. Others were not so lucky.

The 8th of August 1945 saw Maurice hoeing sugar beet and looking forward to the celebrations which heralded the end of the war in Europe, at the aerodrome. He has a continued link with many of the Canadians who were stationed at Skipton-on-Swale airfield, and he still keeps an eye on the memorial which is on the village green.

5th AUGUST 1944 (D/S)
Thirsk Case of Foot and Mouth Disease.
Restrictions in a 15 mile radius.

An outbreak of foot and mouth disease was confirmed on Thursday at the premises of Mr. Percy Lee in Chapel Street, Thirsk. The animals affected were pigs.

THIRSK CASE OF FOOT-AND-MOUTH DISEASE

RESTRICTIONS IN A 15-MILE RADIUS

An outbreak of foot-and-mouth disease was confirmed on Thursday at the premises of Mr. Percy Lee in Chapel-street, Thirsk. The animals affected were pigs.

An area of restriction 15 miles round Thirsk has been declared. In this there can be no movement of stock without licence by the police.

There will be no store markets at Thirsk, Helmsley, Easingwold, Boroughbridge, Ripon, Masham, Bedale, and Northallerton. Collecting centres for fat stock will be authorised at selected points.

An area of restriction 15 miles round Thirsk has been declared. In this there can be no movement of stock without licence by the police. There will be no stock markets at Thirsk, Helmsley, Easingwold, Boroughbridge, Ripon, Masham, Bedale and Northallerton. Collecting centres for fat stock will be authorised at selected points.

14th August 1944 (T.R.D.C.)
War Damage.

Sandhutton:- Several houses sustained broken glass in this village through the explosion of bombs on the Skipton Landing Ground which occurred on the evening of Tuesday, 15th July. I have been verbally informed that this is repairable by the Council as War Damages.

Skipton Bridge:- The crash of a bomber on Saturday afternoon, 5th August, caused damage to three dwelling houses in Skipton Bridge. The Hall, owned and occupied by Dr. Irving has damaged walls, roof and broken glass and woodwork in most of the front windows. A cottage occupied by Jack Meggot received damage to the gable end and front walls and roof. The adjoining cottage occupied by Walter Smith was only slightly damaged, namely a cracked ceiling and cracked sill to front window.

On this Saturday I got two of our employees and protected ground floor windows at the Hall with pluvex. On Monday a re-inspection was made with Mr. Severs and instruction given to make good the damage.

Recommended that the Chairman and Financial officer meet the County Surveyor on the spot to further discuss any necessary further repairs.

24th August 1944

PARIS ENTERED

The bells of Paris were rung to celebrate the beginning of the liberation of the capital of France.

11th September 1944 (T.R.D.C.)
War Damage - Skipton Bridge.

Since the last meeting I have inspected two further cottages owned by Mr. Wm. F. Henderson, which received damage as a result of the Bomber Crash. One occupied by Mr. Sadler, had a first floor front window blown out and brickwork damaged and roof defects. The other, roof defects only.
Sandhutton Damage.

This has now been found to include several damaged ceilings besides broken glass. Instruction has been given for the repair of the above.

13th September 1944 (E.A.M.)

Wellington, Mark 10 : overshot Skipton-on-Swale airfield after attempting to land after one engine failed. Navigation exercise. 200 yards north of Busby Stoop Inn. Crew survived.

16ᵗʰ SEPTEMBER 1944 (D/S)

Thirsk Evening Institute - will re-open on Monday, September 25ᵗʰ. Enrolment at the Secondary School on Friday, September 22ⁿᵈ from 7 to 8.30p.m.

Further particulars from the Organising Master, Mr.F. Holmes, M.Sc.

21ˢᵗ SEPTEMBER 1944

PHILIPPINES ATTACKED

The first American raid on the Philippines. The attack took place from aircraft carriers.

9ᵗʰ OCTOBER 1944 (T.R.D.C.)

Disinfections.:-

The 5 disinfections were all at dwelling houses following cases of infectious diseases - removed to hospital.

Salvage:-

Sales of salvage for the month totalled approximately £45 for the following materials sold:- 4½ tons paper, 8½ cwts of bagging, 6¾ cwts. of mixed rags, 91 doz. bottles and jars and 7cwt. battery lead.

Letter from the Ministry of Health giving notice that factory made temporary houses, housing equipment and demonstration houses were available for inspection. 27ᵗʰ November 1944.

Letter from Mr. A.S. C. Broadway
          A.R.P. Office, Thirsk.
          27ᵗʰ November 1944.

Dear Mr. Gowland,

I understand that you are aware that the Invasion Committees need no longer continue their existence and upon the instructions of the Regional Commissioner I have disbanded the Thirsk and Sowerby Committee with the thanks of the Secretaries of War and Home Security.

At the same time I feel that some word of appreciation should be expressed by the representatives of the district to those gentlemen who served on the Committee for the splendid work and time they gave for our welfare during a most critical and anxious period.

I hope the Council will make some gesture to this end at their next meeting.

In my instructions I was asked to have the records and papers preserved and it is suggested that the Clerk to the District Council would be the appropriate person to take charge of the documents. May I request you to act on the suggestion?

Thank you in anticipation,

A.S.C. Broadway

District Controller and Chairman Invasion Committee.

Resolved.:-

That the Council place on record their appreciation of the excellent services rendered by members of the Invasion Committee viz:- Inspector Crawford, Dr. W.G. MacArthur, Lt. Gooding, Messrs Holmes and W.A. Wilkinson under the Chairmanship of Mr. A.S.C.Broadway.

Evacuation.

Mr. E. Reed (Hon. Billeting Officer) reported that all evacuees with the exception of those in the London area had now returned to their homes.

Resolved that the Council place on record the excellent services rendered by Mr. E. Reed in carrying out the Evacuation Scheme.

4th DECEMBER 1944 (E.A.M.)

Halifax, Mark 2 : flew into Whitestonecliffe at 22.10 hours practising low level night bombing. Five crew killed, 2 injured.

CHAPTER NINE
1945

14th JANUARY 1945 (E.A.M.)

Halifax, Mark 3 : crashed into top edge of Whitestonecliffe (21.15 hours). Pilot and five other Canadians killed. Rear gunner injured - rescued by a local civilian who was awarded a medal for his efforts.

15th JANUARY 1945 (E.A.M.)

Halifax, Mark 3 : on route from Topcliffe Airfield crashed at Mount St.John at 20.58 hours flying circuits and landing after takeoff at 20.55 hours. Duration of flight only 3 minutes. Crew of 9 all killed in crash.

18th JANUARY 1945

BUDAPEST FALLS

62,000 German troops surrendered to the Allies following the capture of Budapest.

1st FEBRUARY 1945

TODAY IS NEW COUPON DAY

Today is new coupon day and there are 24 new clothes coupons. The Board of Trade warn us not to be in a rush spending them. They might have to last seven months instead of six. That means 3½ coupons per month instead of four. There are smaller stocks to meet those millions of new coupons than there has been at any period in the war. Wholesale and retail stocks are at their lowest level.

The Board of Trade feels that at the moment there are enough goods in the shops to meet the public's coupons. It will depend on the extent of those stocks whether our coupons will have to last until September instead of August. Shops are expecting the biggest coupon expenditure on stockings. Extreme shortage of coupons has been noticed during the past few weeks by the number of women braving the severe weather in bare legs.

3rd FEBRUARY 1945 (D/S)

The greatest snowfall and freeze-up for years came to an end on Monday night. There had been about eleven days of continuous frost following heavy snow, many villages being cut off by deep drifts from which buses and even railway trains had to be dug out. Burst water pipes became epidemic, and the few plumbers available have many months work ahead in making repairs.

12th FEBRUARY 1945 (T.R.D.C.)

Nuisances found included the following matters.

Foul and dilapidated privy midden dangerous and over-hanging wall at premises situated Three Tuns Hotel, Market Place, Thirsk, in occupation by the Military. This originated as a complaint from the military to the County Medical Officer, but as the nuisance is on registered property the Military Authorities have agreed to remedy.

Salvage.

Owing to the bad weather and lack of transport, no salvage was sold during the month.

Heather Schroeter.

Heather's first memory of Thirsk at war was of soldiers of the Territorial Army marching down Chapel Street, and waving them off.

After attending Sowerby School and suffering, as did others, from the knuckles of Miss Hunt, Heather started work at Reedman's Bakery aged fourteen. Prior to this she had worked part-time in the kitchens of The Golden Fleece Hotel. The family lived at World's End but then moved to a house in Villa Place. Horse and traps dominated Thirsk Market Place during the early years of the war.

Heather became a member of the Auxiliary Fire Service, (the A.F.S.) as a telephonist. She was on duty twice a week from eight in the evening until seven the next morning. Bunks were available for sleep during the quieter periods. The calls to the A.F.S. were mainly concerned with plane crashes. With being in the A.F.S. Heather was issued with two gas masks - a civilian one and a service type. When issued with the latter she had to undergo a gas test by walking through a gas chamber wearing her service gas mask. An eerie experience. After duty with the fire service it was immediately back to work.

Along with so many other young girls Heather loved dancing. She and her friends would often walk to Knayton Village Hall for a dance. Dances in the Parochial Hall at Sowerby and Thirsk Town Hall finished by ten thirty. She enjoyed several dances, e.g. waltz, foxtrot, quickstep and the Gay Gordons. Recreation could also be found at the local cinema watching stars such as Greer Garson in Mrs Miniver. The newsreels showed what was happening in the global conflict.

If the opportunity arose Heather and her friend travelled by train to York on a Saturday afternoon. They had to save up only to find the trains packed with troops. Expeditions like this required clothing coupons and money and the two girls had neither. In spite of the black-out Heather was confident when she was out in the evening and did not need a torch, even if she could have bought a battery for it. She became familiar with the different sounds of aeroplane engines and on her way home one night with some friends a bomb dropped as she was coming off the Green. Fortunately some soldiers pushed her into a doorway for protection. She still ran all the way home!

The army was looking after the prisoners of war at Thirkleby and the Sergeants used to hold a dance in their mess. An Army wagon would be sent down to the Market Place to transport the girls to the dance. These dances were always good fun.

Thirsk's Auxiliary Fire Service 12th February 1945

Thirsk was a quiet, sleepy market town where everybody knew everybody else. Rationing seemed to present no real problems for there were plenty of farms nearby who could provide most things. One of Heather's abiding memories of wartime is when she went with an aunt for a week's holiday at West Hartlepool. The week seemed to be spent in an Anderson shelter with the family they were staying with.

Shrapnel frequently hit the roof of the shelter and a huge bomb crater in the field next to the house had to be seen to be believed. A post card was sent home every day to say to a worried family in Thirsk that they were all right.

Heather was eventually conscripted and was posted to Middlesbrough for a six week training course. She was billeted in local lodgings and because of her bakery experience was sent to work in a canteen at a Norton aircraft factory. Here she learned how to cater for a lot of people. From Norton she was posted to Sheffield and was billeted in a Nissen hut. Here she prepared food for Bevin Boys (miners), who lived in a miner's hostel. She had one day off a week and if she saved up for her days off she was able to come home for a short spell.

When V.E. Day was announced, (8th May, 1945), Heather and her friend Vera, with ten shillings between them, set off for London. They ended up watching the celebrations in Tottenham Court Road. Buskers abounded and in the parade they spotted a lad from Thirsk. The crowds were such that they tied their coats together to prevent them becoming separated. The exhausted pair returned to Thirsk after almost twenty four hours in the capital. A fitting end to the war in Europe.

Peter Schroeter.

Peter left school in April 1940 aged fourteen. He trained as an air-frame mechanic in Leipzig, Germany for the next three and a half years. The impact of the German advance across Europe was not noticeable at first apart from rationing and shortages. Peter's mother and sister were evacuated as Allied Bombing on German targets increased. The 3rd and 4th December saw the heaviest raid when Leipzig was pulverised.

On the 6th January 1944 Peter was conscripted into what was known as the Labour Service. His work at this time was in agriculture. This type of work continued for six months when he was transferred to the German rocket centre at Peenemunde. Five days after D-Day he received his final and proper call up papers. He was ordered to report to Kauf-Beuren in the south of Germany where he underwent basic training. Following this he was transported by train to Holland and was involved in the fighting at Arnhem.

Shortly after this bloody battle Peter was taken prisoner and was transported to a transit camp at Dieppe. From here he was shipped across the Channel to Kempton Park. Whilst at Kempton Park he was interrogated and assessed for work. From Kempton Park he was sent to a tented camp in Sheffield. The camp was surrounded by coils of barbed wire and guarded by the military. There was little to do apart from loitering and talking. Peter could speak some English and he used his skill in helping his fellow prisoners. Bartering became a way of life in such camps. Watches, rings, toys made by the prisoners, were exchanged for cigarettes and food. One of the prisoners made a football by tying rags together and as long as the ball lasted a game would be played.

When the war ended the prisoners were dispersed and assigned to agricultural work. Peter worked on farms in the Ripon, Driffield, Sedgefield areas until he ended up in Thirkleby P.O.W. Camp. This was still guarded. For a time Peter worked for Squire Bell and did whatever was required.

Peter, along with some other prisoners continued to work in the locality of Thirsk. During one outing he met Heather who was on her way to the Kilburn Feast. They were married in March 1948 and he became a British citizen.

26th MARCH 1945 (T.R.D.C.)

Letter from the Topcliffe Parish meeting asking that some arrangements be made for the removal of corpses in the area.

Resolved that this be discussed at the next meeting of the Sanitary Plans and Housing Committee.

PRESIDENT ROOSEVELT DIES

President Roosevelt, President of the United States of America, died during his fourth term of office. He was succeeded by Harry S. Truman.

15th APRIL 1945

BELSEN HORRORS

Evidence of mass murder by the Germans on an unbelievable scale - a total of 35,000 corpses were counted at Belsen Concentration Camp and this was only one of the Nazi's extermination camps.

28th APRIL 1945

MUSSOLINI SHOT DEAD

The day after Mussoloni's death all German troops in Italy surrendered unconditionally.

1st MAY 1945

10.30 p.m. The BBC's Home Service was interrupted by the voice of Stuart Hibberd broadcasting from Glasgow.

'This is London calling. Here is a news flash. The German radio has just announced that Hitler is dead.'

7th MAY 1945 (T.R.D.C.)

Letter from the Ministry of Works in regard to Prisoner of War Camp Water Supply stating that they were fitting a new pressure sustaining valve as soon as possible.

7th MAY 1945

The Board of Trade announcement:- Until the end of May you may buy cotton bunting without coupons, as long as it is red, white and blue and does not cost more than one shilling and threepence per square yard.

MINISTRY OF FUEL AND POWER.

COAL SUPPLIES.
1st May, 1945—30th April, 1946.

In order to secure the most equitable distribution of the supplies of coal likely to be available, the following restrictions relating to controlled premises will operate from the 1st May, 1945 to the 30th April, 1946:—

I. HOUSE AND KITCHEN COAL AND COALITE.
   THE MAXIMUM QUANTITY FOR THE 12 MONTHS IS 50 CWT., of which not more than 10 cwt. may be obtained (except under licence) in each of the three-month periods commencing 1st May and 1st August and not more than 10 cwt. in any of the two-month periods commencing 1st November, 1st January and 1st March.

II. COKE, ANTHRACITE, WELSH DRY STEAM COAL, AND ALL MANUFACTURED FUELS OTHER THAN COALITE.
    THE MAXIMUM QUANTITY FOR THE 12 MONTHS IS 40 CWT., of which not more than 20 cwt. may be obtained (except under licence) in each of the two periods, May—October and November—April (inclusive).

Consumers who have need of larger supplies in either group, because they are entirely dependant on solid fuel or have special needs, should apply to the Local Fuel Overseer at the address given below. Early application is advisable.

Licences may also be granted by Fuel Overseers, if the supply situation permits, to enable consumers to stock during the Summer, a larger proportion of the year's supply without allowing any additional quantity for the year as a whole.

III. The following fuels may be obtained free of restriction provided supplies are available locally:—

Unscreened coke breeze, washery slurry, anthracite grains, duff and large, Welsh dry steam large, and bituminous fines not exceeding one-eighth of an inch.

DON'T BURN COAL UNNECESSARILY DURING THE SUMMER OR EARLY AUTUMN. STOCK COAL NOW WITHIN THE LIMITS ALLOWED, BUT KEEP YOUR STOCK FOR THE REAL WINTER WEATHER. ADDITIONAL SUPPLIES WILL NOT BE MADE AVAILABLE LATER.

Issued by:—
A. J. DURSTON, Local Fuel Overseer, Richmond M.B.
H. W. BOANAS, Local Fuel Overseer, Richmond R.D.
G. BARNINGHAM, Local Fuel Overseer, Richmond R.D.
S. F. ESLAND, Local Fuel Overseer, Northallerton Urban.
H. TEMPLEMAN, Local Fuel Overseer, Northallerton Rural.
H. PRESTON, Local Fuel Overseer, Aysgarth Rural.
J. W. HEDDON, Local Fuel Overseer, Bedale Rural.
G. W. WETHERELL, Local Fuel Overseer, Leyburn Rural.
J. W. HEDDON, Local Fuel Overseer, Masham Rural.
F. METCALFE, Local Fuel Overseer, Thirsk Rural.
W. C. EDEN, Local Fuel Overseer, Wath Rural.

8th MAY 1945

RANGOON LIBERATED

The Japanese in the Pacific abandoned Rangoon following heavy bombing raids.

8th MAY 1945

GERMANY SURRENDERS

Victory in Europe Day took place on the 8th May 1945. The war in Europe ended with the unconditional surrender of all German forces to the Allied Command. Peoples in the cities, towns and villages of Europe rejoiced that in Europe, at least, the war is over.

Arrangements for V.E. Day (T.R.D.C.)
Circular letter from the Home Office.

His Majesty's Government have had under consideration the way in which the defeat of the enemy in Europe should be celebrated. The end of the war in Europe will not be the end of the struggle and there should be no relaxation of the national effort until the war in the Far East has been won. It will, however, be the general desire of the nation to celebrate the victorious end of the European campaigns before turning with renewed energy to the completion of the tasks before it.

Accordingly as already announced, the day on which the cessation of organised resistance is announced, which will generally be known as V.E. Day, and the day following, will be public holidays. The cessation of hostilities in Europe will be announced by the Prime Minister over the wireless and His Majesty the King will address his people throughout the world at nine p.m. the same day. It is the wish of his Majesty the King that the Sunday following V.E. Day should be observed as a day of thanksgiving and prayer.

Except in the coastal areas in which dim-out or black-out restrictions are still maintained they will, however, raise no objection to the use on V.E. night or the succeeding night by local authorities and public bodies of such flood-lighting as exist and can be brought into use. In addition the Armed Forces will make available for illumination purposes such lighting as can be spared.

Bonfires will be allowed, but the government trust that the paramount necessity of ensuring that only material with no salvage value is used and the desirability of proper arrangements with the National Fire Service to guard against any possible spread of fire will be borne in mind by those arranging bonfires.

In view of the pressure on public transport generally throughout the country it seems to the government desirable that facilities for indoor entertainment should be available as widely as possible. They would not suggest that theatres, music halls and cinemas should remain open later than the hours prevailing before V.E. Day, but, provided that adequate staffs can be made available, they hope that the arrangements of theatres, music halls and cinemas will keep their premises open until the usual hour.

As regard premises licensed for public dancing, the government think that these might be allowed to remain open later than the normal closing hour.

Licensing authorities for the sale of intoxicating liquors are already approving applications from license holders for special orders of exemption, or special permission in respect of V.E. Day, from the requirements as to the permitted hours. His Majesty's government suggest that advance individual applications for special orders of exemption or special permission for an extension of the evening permitted hours on V.E. Day should receive sympathetic consideration in the light of local circumstances.

No exemptions should be granted in respect of the afternoon 'break', nor should applications be entertained in general for any special order of exemption or special permission on the day following V.E. Day.

In that the essential requirements of the public be met, the government recommend that businesses selling and distributing food should remain open for a few hours on V.E. Day to enable the public to get supplies and, subject to maintaining the sale or delivery of essential commodities such as bread, milk and rations, close on the following day. They appreciate this will mean some inconvenience to those engaged in these essential services, though it is understood holidays in lieu will be granted under trade agreements. On Thanksgiving Sunday His Majesty's Government think it appropriate that local authorities should organise victory parades either with the local Service of Thanksgiving or later in the day.

In addition to such representation of the Armed Forces as can be arranged with the local commander, the local authorities will no doubt wish to include all those associated with the wide range of the Civil Defence Services, The National Fire Service, the Fire Guard, the Police, The Women's Land Army, war workers of all categories, and members of various youth organisations and voluntary societies.

King's Speech.

At nine o'clock in the evening King George V1 spoke to his people on the wireless. 'Today we give thanks to Almighty God for a great deliverance. Speaking from our Empire's oldest capital city, war-battered but never for one moment daunted or dismayed, speaking from London, I ask you to join with me in that act of thanksgiving. Germany, the enemy who drove all Europe into war, has been finally overcome. In the Far East we have yet to deal with the Japanese, a determined and cruel foe. To this we shall turn with the utmost resolve and with all our resources. But at this hour, when the dreadful shadow of war has passed from our hearts and homes in these islands, we may at last make one pause for thanksgiving.

Let us think what it was that upheld us through nearly six years of suffering and peril.

The knowledge that everything was at stake, our freedom, our independence, our very existence as a people; but the knowledge also that in defending ourselves we were defending the liberties of the whole world; that our cause was the cause, not of this nation only, not of this Empire and Commonwealth only, but of every land where freedom is cherished and law and liberty go hand in hand. In the darkest hours we knew that the enslaved and isolated peoples of Europe looked to us; their hopes were our hopes; their confidence confirmed our faith. We knew that, if we failed, the last remaining barrier against a world-wide tyranny would have fallen into ruins. But we did not fail. We kept our faith with ourselves and with one another; we kept faith with our great allies. That faith and unity have carried us through to victory.

There is great comfort in the thought that the years of darkness and danger in which the children of our country have grown up are over and, please God, for ever. We shall have failed, and the blood of our dearest will have flowed in vain, if the victory which they died to win does not lead to a lasting peace, founded on justice and established in good will.

To this then, let us turn our thoughts on this day of just triumph and proud sorrow.'

(B.B.C.Archives)

12th MAY 1945 (D/S)

Thanksgiving Services Precede Rejoicings. Crowded congregations at thanksgiving services, beflagged houses, open air dancing, bonfires, children's sports, street parties were features of V.E. celebrations.

19th MAY 1945

Thirsk.

Saturday, May 26th 1945.

Clay Pigeon Shoot.

In aid of Welcome Home Funds

Open Events   Farmer's Event.

Local Event   Keeper's Event

Valuable prizes for all Events.

Commence 1.15 p.m.

24th MAY 1945

TOKYO BOMBED

Tokyo, capital of Japan, was successfully bombed this day.

11ᵗʰ June 1945 (T.R.D.C.)

Letter from the Ministry of Works stating that they had informed the Camp Commandant of Thirkleby Prisoner of War Camp to turn on the water at 10p.m. at night and off at 6 a.m. in the morning.

25ᵗʰ June 1945 (T.R.D.C.)

Letter from the Quartering Commandant of the Royal Signals, stating that they were not in a position to release the Sutton Road Housing Site.

Winding up Civil Defence.

The District Controller, (Mr. A.S.C. Broadway) submitted copy of a letter which had been addressed to all members of the Civil Defence notifying them of the official winding up on 1ˢᵗ July next and thanking them for their past services.

The Hon. Billeting Officer, (Mr. E. Reed), reported that on Monday last, the last of the Official Evacuees had returned to London and that with the exception of the dispersal of equipment, evacuation had come to an end.

26ᵗʰ July 1945

CHURCHILL DEFEATED - ATTLEE NOW PRIME MINISTER

Following the results of a General Election, Winston Churchill tendered his resignation and Clement Attlee became Prime Minister of a Labour Government which had a clear majority over other parties.

29ᵗʰ July 1945

AMERICAN CRUISER 'INDIANAPOLIS' LOST

The American cruiser 'Indianapolis' was torpedoed. Some 883 men lost their lives in this attack by the Japanese. Unknown to the Japanese, the 'Indianapolis' had completed her mission of delivering to Tinian Island the atomic bomb.

6ᵗʰ August 1945

ATOMIC BOMB DROPPED ON HIROSHIMA

A B.29 bomber the Enola Gay, dropped an atomic bomb on the Japanese city of Hiroshima. Some 80,000 died and 35,000 injured as a result of this bombing raid.

9ᵗʰ August 1945

ATOMIC BOMB DROPPED ON NAGASAKI

The Japanese had still not surrendered unconditionally. A specially adapted B.29 bomber, Bock's Car, with orders to drop the second atomic bomb on Kokura. Kokura was obscured by cloud and Nagasaki was the second choice. 40,000 people were killed and this number was to rise to 49,000 in the days following the dropping of the bomb.

14ᵗʰ AUGUST 1945
UNCONDITIONAL SURRENDER OF JAPAN

15ᵗʰ AUGUST 1945
PEACE ON EARTH

The Prime Minister, Mr. Attlee, said, 'Let us recall that on December 7ᵗʰ 1941, Japan, whose onslaught China had already resisted for over four years, fell upon the United States of America, and upon ourselves, who were so oppressed in our death struggles with Germany and Italy.

Taking full advantage of surprise and treachery, the Japanese forces quickly over-ran the territories of ourselves and our allies in the Far East, and at one time it appeared as though these invaders would reach the mainland of Australia and advance into India. But the tide turned, first slowly then with ever increasing speed and violence, as mighty forces of the United States and the British Commonwealth and Empire and of course our allies, and finally Russia, were brought to bear.

Their resistance has now everywhere been broken. At this time we should pay tribute to the men from this country, from the Dominions, from India and the colonies, to our allied armies and air forces that have fought so well against Japan.

Our gratitude goes out to all our splendid allies, above all to the United States, without whose prodigious efforts this war in the East would have many years to run.

We also think especially at this time of the prisoners in Japanese hands, of our friends in the Dominions, Australia and New Zealand, in India and Burma and in those colonial territories upon whom the brunt of the Japanese attack fell.

We rejoice that their sufferings will soon be at an end and that these territories will soon be purged of the Japanese invaders.

Here at home you have earned rest from the increasing efforts you have all borne, without complaint, through so many dark years. I have no doubt throughout industry generally the Government's lead in the matter of victory holidays will be followed and that tomorrow, Wednesday, and Thursday will everywhere be treated as days of holiday.

There are some who must necessarily remain at work on these days to maintain essential services, and I am sure they can be relied on to carry on.

When we return to work on Friday morning we must turn again to the great tasks before us. But, for the moment, let all who can relax and enjoy themselves in the knowledge of work well done.

Peace has once again come to the world. Let us thank God for His great deliverance and His mercies. Long live the King.'

A Selection of Wartime Songs

Wish Me Luck As You Wave Me Goodbye

Hang Out The Washing On The Seigfried Line

Run Rabbit, Run Rabbit Run

Coming In On A Wing and a Prayer

When They Sound The Last All Clear

Whistle While You Work

White Cliffs of Dover

Kiss Me Goodnight Sergeant Major

Roll Out the Barrel

If You Were The Only Girl In The World

We'll Meet Again

Long Ago and Far Away

Don't Sit Under the Apple Tree

Lilli Marlene

Don't Get Around Much Any More

Many lyrics were made up by children. The following lyric was sung to the tune of 'Whistle While You Work.'

Whistle while you work

Hitler is a twerp

Hitler's barmy, so's his army,

Whistle while you work.

Sources

Darlington and Stockton Times. (D/S)

Northern Echo.

Evening Chronicle.

Minutes of Thirsk Rural District Council (T.R.D.C.)

Records Office, Northallerton.

Diary of Neil Graham 1941-1943

Darlington Library.

Thirsk Library.

Aerodromes in North Yorkshire, and Wartime
Memories-David Brown.

Second World War : Martin Gilbert (Wedenfield & Nicolson)

The People's War : Angus Calder (Jonathan Cape)

No Time to Wave Good-bye : Ben Wicks (Bloomsbury)

British Women Go to War : J.B. Priestley (Collins)

Evacuation : Bob Holman (Lion Publishing)

They Fought in the Fields : Nicola Tyrer (Sinclair-Stevenson)

Elvington Air Museum.

Memorial Room - RAF Linton-on-Ouse

Eden Camp.

Thirsk Museum.

Acknowledgements

Thanks are due to the many people who shared their wartime memories with me. These include Maurice Sanderson, Jean Cave, Peter and Heather Schroeter, J.Terry Barker, Dave Brown, Frank Smith, Bill Rukin, Jim Burns, Ray Ballard, Neil Graham, Bessie Hart, Joyce Appleton, Stan and Margaret Josephs, Laurie Jackson, Chris Wright, May Wyon, Kay Konieczny, Jack Moss, Jack Severs, Don Fothergill, Myra Otterburn, Ken Wright, Edna Garbutt, Rose Stothard, Bob Smith, Richard Chapman, Hilda Chapman, Olga Brown, J.E. Moores, Roger Bibby, Ann Nelson, Ann Coates, Don Collinson, Cooper Harding, John Bennett, J. Coldwell, Muriel Skene, Norah Forster, Elizabeth Clarke, Rita Hodgson, Maurice Ormston, Pearl Marshall, Jane Rowntree.

To all of these people I wish to express my thanks.

Geoff. Moore.
Thirsk 2004.

CHRONOLOGY

1918	First World War ends : Germany defeated.
1921	Hitler becomes leader of the National Socialist Party.
1930	Nazi Party gains election success in Germany.
1933	Hitler appointed Chancellor and the persecution of the Jews continues.
1934	Hitler takes the title Fuhrer.
1935	Treaty of Versaille broken by Hitler as Germany begins to re-arm.
1936	Spanish Civil War begins.
1937	British budget provides a National Defence Contribution.
	Hitler in support of Franco in the Spanish Civil War sends the Condor Legion of the Lufftwaffe to Guernica to try out the new tactic of blanket bombing.
1938	All British school children to be issued with gas masks. Germany announces union with Austria.
	In Britain car manufacturers switch to aircraft production.
	The Czechoslovakian territory of Sudetenland handed over to Germany.
	Neville Chamberlain, British Prime Minister, returns from a meeting with Hitler and claims it is 'Peace for our time.'
	Sir John Anderson becomes responsible for Air Raid Precautions (A.R.P) and begins to plan for evacuation.
1939	In Britain over one million people volunteer for Civil Defence.duties.

1939 cont.	National Registration list enables a register of the whole population to be created prior to the issuing of Identity Cards.
	I.R.A (Irish Republican Army) continues its bombing campaign on mainland Britain.
	Germany invades Czechoslovakia contrary to Munich Agreement.
24th August	Emergency Powers Defence Act passed. Compulsory conscription for men aged twenty and twenty one.
25th August	Treaty of Alliance between Poland and Britain signed.
	Emergency Powers Act giving government powers regarding security, public safety, industry and the requisitioning of land and property.
September	Conscription of males extended to forty-one years of age.
	Suspension of raising of school leaving age.
1st Sept.	Poland invaded by German troops.
	Evacuation of children, the blind and expectant mothers begins.
	Blackout enforced and thousands of patients discharged from hospitals to make way for casualties expected from air-raids.
3rdSept.	War declared by Britain on Germany.
	Cinemas, theatres and places of public entertainment closed.
	Gas masks to be carried at all times, and BBC closes all channels except the Home Service.
4th Sept.	Beginning of 'phoney war' - no German bombardment on England.
17th Sept.	Russia invades Poland.
November	National Savings Movement launched.

1939 cont.

23rd Nov.   This is the last date to register for ration books.

December   Many evacuees return home and places of public
                 entertainment begin to re-open.

1940

8th January   Food rationing begins : 4 oz.bacon, 4 oz,ham, 12 oz.sugar,
                 4 oz.butter - all per person per week.

March   Meat rationing begins : 1s.10d worth a week for adults and
                 11d for children.

3rd April   Lord Woolton becomes Minister of Food.

9th April   Norway and Denmark invaded by Germany.

10th May   Germany invades Belgium, Holland, Luxembourg, France
                 and Holland.

                 Chamberlain resigns. Churchill becomes Prime Minister.

13th May   Churchill rallies the nation with his 'blood, sweat and tears'
                 speech.

14th May   Appeal for Local Defence Volunteers (renamed Home
                 Guard).

15th May   Holland surrenders.

22nd May   Emergency Powers Act passed giving government absolute
                 authority over property and British population.

28th May   Belgium surrenders.

29th May - 4th June

                 Evacuation of British and Allied forces from Dunkirk.

                 Aircraft workers working seventy hour week over seven days.

Lord Beaverbrook, Minister of Aircraft Production, appeals for scrap metal.

July   Tea, margarine, and cooking fats rationed to 2oz.per week. Cheese ration fluctuates.

10th July - 17th October

Battle of Britain by R.A.F.

7th Sept.   Blitz begins on London. Londoners take refuge in underground stations.

15th Sept.   Heavy air-raids on London, Cardiff, Southampton, Manchester, Bristol, Liverpool.

12th Oct.   Operation Sealion (Germany's invasion of Britain) postponed.

4th Dec.   Offensive against Italians begins in North Africa.

1941

22nd Jan.   Tobruk in North Africa captured by British and Australian forces.

March   Registration of Employment Order for women 20-21, later extended to 30 and men over 41.

Preserves, margarine, treacles, etc., rationed to maximum of 8oz. per month.

5th March   Essential Work Order required all skilled workers to register and to move to more essential work if instructed.

April   National Service Act allows for all citizens to be liable for military service.

May   Cheese ration down to 1oz.per week.

1st June   Clothes rationing introduced.

1941 cont

22nd June	Germany invades Russia.
June	Utility Scheme introduced for retail goods.
July	Some 30,000 men conscripted to work in mines.
November	Controlled distribution of milk.
7th Dec.	Japanese attack American Pacific Fleet at Pearl Harbour.
8th Dec.	U.S.A. and Britain declare war on Japan.
9th Dec.	Conscription for single women between 20 and 30.
	War work now compulsory.
	Conscription age for men raised to 50.
11th Dec.	U.S.A declares war on Germany and Italy.

1942

January	'Wings for Victory' weeks held across the country.
February	American military (GIs) arrive in the United Kingdom.
15th Feb.	Fall of Singapore.
March	Fuel stocks very low - rationing of fuel discussed in House of Commons.
23rd April	Bombing of historic cathedral cities.
June	Decorated domestic crockery banned. Such crockery only to be available in plain white.
21st June	Rommel takes Tobruk.
July	Sweet rationing introduced.

August	Utility Scheme restricts furniture to twenty-two basic items.
	Montgomery takes command of the 8th Army in North Africa.
October - November	
	Battle of El Alamein - Germans retreat.
	Church bells ring throughout Britain in celebration of victory in Egypt.
17th Dec.	Nazis mass extermination of Jewish people results in statement in House of Commons.

1943

January	No unemployment.
	Some 300,000 savings groups in action.
18th Jan.	German Luftwaffe resumes raids on Britain.
March - September	
	Major offensive by Bomber Command against German towns.
16-17th May	Dambusters raid.
July	Fuel, petrol, food, blankets, beer, continue to be scarce.
9th July	Allies invade Sicily.
3rd Sept.	Allies invade Italy.
13th Oct.	Italy declares war on Germany.
December	One million women in trade unions.

1944   'Salute the Soldier' weeks held across the country.

January   Fuel very scarce - only 4cwt coal allowed per month.

                Divorce made easier by suspension of three-year cooling off period.

                Beginning of 'Little Blitz' on London.

March   Bomber Command continues offensive over Germany.

4th June   Allies enter Rome.

6th June   D-Day. Allied forces land in Normandy.

13th June   V1 flying bomb hits London.

25th Aug.   Liberation of Paris.

8th Sept.   V2 rocket attack on Britain.

17th Sept.   Blackout replaced by Dim-out.

20th Oct.   First German town, Aachen, in Allied hands.

December   Home Guard stood down.

1945

27th Jan.   Auschwitz concentration camp liberated.

4-12th Feb.   Yalta Conference when Churchill, Roosevelt, and Stalin met to discuss how they will deal with Germany and Japan when the war has ended.

13th Feb.   The German city of Dresden is destroyed by bombing.

29th March   Last V1 launched at Britain.

13th April   Belsen and Buchenwald (German concentration camps) liberated.

30th April	Hitler commits suicide.
4th May	Britain captures Rangoon in Burma.
7th May	Unconditional surrender of German forces.
8th May	VE Day - Victory in Europe celebrated.
26th July	Churchill defeated at polls. Attlee leads a Labour Government.
6th Aug.	USA drops atomic bomb on Hiroshima.
9th Aug.	USA drops second atomic bomb on Nagasaki.
14th Aug.	Unconditional surrender of Japan.
15th Aug.	VJ Day (Victory over Japan)